SRA
Corrective Reading
Decoding B1   Decoding Strategies

Differentiated Reinforcement Fluency Program

Siegfried Engelmann

Donald Crawford

Tina Wells

Mc
Graw
Hill
Education

Acknowledgments

Corrective Reading Differentiated Reinforcement Fluency Program is based on materials written by Siegfried Engelmann, Linda Carnine, Gary Johnson, Linda Meyer, Wesley Becker, and Julie Eisele for *Corrective Reading.*

Cover Photo: BlueMoon Stock/SuperStock

MHEonline.com

Send all inquiries to:
McGraw-Hill Education
8787 Orion Place
Columbus, OH 43240

ISBN: 978-0-07-623522-3
MHID: 0-07-623522-X

Printed in the United States of America.

11 12 13 14 15 16 LHN 21 20

Contents

Contents

SRA Differentiated Reinforcement Fluency

Decoding B1

PART 1: Teacher's Guide

PART 1: TEACHER'S GUIDE

Differentiated Reinforcement Fluency Program—*Decoding B1*

Differentiated reinforcement means that there is more than one level of reinforcement. In this program, there is some reinforcement of a student's average performance. However, there is even stronger reinforcement of performances that are above the student's average performance.

Problems with Popular Fluency Improvement Strategies

Teaching most discriminations or skills requires designing the instructional program so it satisfies multiple criteria. The lower the performance level of the learners, the more carefully the various criteria must be designed if the learners are to learn exactly what you expect the learners to learn. Instruction that does not address the full range of criteria is sloppy, and learners will often learn something other than what the teacher intended to teach.

"Teaching" reading fluency to low performers (students in the first quartile) is an example of the delicate balance among the various criteria.

Poor Practices—Examples

Often the instruction focuses on one criterion at the expense of others when a balanced approach is needed. For example, a teacher wants to increase the reading rate of low performers, so she introduces a plan that focuses on the reading rate but that does not take into account the role of reinforcement, the "difficulty" of the material students are to read, and the interplay between rate and accuracy. Here are some possible scenarios.

Approach 1 For this approach, the teacher requires the learners to read passages aloud. The teacher records the time. Some learners improve sporadically, but because the program does not address the difficulty level of the various passages learners practice, the performance does not follow a progressive trend. One day the teacher observes possible improvement, but the next day shows serious regression.

So the implication is that the selections must be arranged so they increase in difficulty slowly and progressively. Learners receive mixed messages if their performance is up one day and down the next.

Approach 2 The teacher may conclude that performance will be less spotty if the reading material is composed of the same bank of words. When such material is used, lower performers improve more predictably from one selection to the next, but when performance is measured over several months, the teacher often discovers that the learners are not improving over time.

Approach 3 Next, the teacher tries something like precision teaching, which includes some form of reinforcement for improvement. Students chart their daily performance. The charts show how many words per minute the learners read. This provision makes it clear to the learners that their reading rate is supposed to improve.

Indeed, the teacher observes improvement in rate. Students are definitely reading faster. When somebody analyzes the data for errors, however, it turns out that the learners improved only in rate. The reading mistakes that were made when the material was read more slowly still occur at the same frequency. The students read more words per minute, but they make the same proportion of errors and the same kinds of errors (omitting words, misreading words, adding words). For example, a learner confuses the words "a" and "the" on 55% of the occasions when reading at the rate of 32 words per minute. When the learner reads at 50 words per minute, "a" and "the" are confused on 57% of their occurrences. So even though the percentages of mistakes are not greatly different, the reading is worse now than it was at the slower rate.

Approach 4 Next, the teacher tries repeating readings of the same passage until a particular rate is achieved. This rate is based on **correct** words per minute, which means that the learners must read both at a higher rate and fairly accurately.

The teacher counts the words read accurately on the initial reading of the passage and then counts the number of words read accurately on subsequent readings. If the teacher establishes a goal of reading 60 correct words per minute, students reread the passage until they achieve this rate. Then the teacher introduces the next passage.

The teacher discovers that indeed the learner shows improvement with multiple rereadings of the passage. The first time the learner reads the passage, the rate of reading is around 30 words per minute, but after the fourth or fifth reading, it has climbed to more than 50 words per minute. Furthermore, the learner makes a smaller percentage of mistakes than on the first reading. After the tenth reading, learners tend to read the passage at about 60 words per minute.

Teachers who use this procedure for a few months frequently observe that the rate of the learners' first reading of a new passage does not show consistent improvement over the first-reading performance of the previous passage. The learners continue to make mistakes about as frequently on the first reading and read at about the same rate as earlier first readings. Typically learners improve no faster on first readings than they improved earlier. Although the data seems to show that learners become more accurate the more times they read a

passage, the reason tends not to be that their reading accuracy has improved, simply that they have become more familiar with the passage and have memorized parts of it. So in the end, this procedure does not really reinforce learners for reading more accurately, simply for trying to memorize the material.

There are two reasons that repeated readings is a poor strategy for improving fluency. One is that it sends the wrong message about the learner's competence. The other is that the training makes the learner depend on multiple readings to read with better fluency. The overall message the teacher communicates to the learner is: "You're a poor reader. You can see that others can read fluently without rereading and rereading. You, however, need multiple readings."

Now the pressure is on. The students have to read faster, so the teacher goes back to single readings and tells the children that they *must* improve. "Read faster," she urges, and they try. They frown, clench their fists, try to make their voices go faster, which results in more self-corrects and rereading, but their improvement is slight. In fact some of the children do a higher percentage of self-corrects and make a higher percentage of mistakes than they did before the "get tough" procedure was instituted. The net result for most of the children is that reading makes them nervous, and they develop various superstitious behaviors, like clearing their throats, saying things like "I mean . . . ," and repeatedly glancing at the teacher to see if her face gives clues about the quality of the reading.

In the end, the teacher is left with the sorry conclusion that some students can't seem to do it. Higher performers read like machines, spitting out more than 150 words per minute, while lower students fit the universal description of "struggling.

Somebody points out that the procedures are simply frustrating the low performers. The teacher finally realizes that there is not a significant payoff for the time and effort she and the children put into fluency practice, so she changes her strategy to a soft sell. Instead of insisting that children read faster, she simply lets them read aloud, with the hope they will read faster when they are "ready." Although the teacher corrects most of the mistakes students make, they tend not to improve quickly because they are apparently "not ready."

Why Is Faster Reading Rate Important?

The first thing you must recognize is that the low performers are not reading faster because they can't. They certainly know what you want them to do; they see that you and other children can do it. Those who try very hard show all the symptoms of exerting serious physical energy. They simply can't do it.

The next thing to recognize is that these children can improve in reading. Although they can't improve as rapidly as the higher-performing children, they are able to learn to read orally at nearly the same rate they speak or hear language. No, it is not about training Jennifer to spit out words at the rate of 180 per minute (which is a ridiculously fast oral rate) or training Brad to read without any apparent concern for the material aside from the sound and number of words he can recite in one minute.

The idea behind appropriate oral-reading rate is to attain a rate that is close to that of spoken language. If students read so slowly that it takes them three or four times as long to decode a sentence as it would if somebody said the sentence at a normal rate, great strain is put on the students' memory. Because it takes longer for students to complete the sentence, they must hold the words in memory a lot longer than they would if they read at a normal speaking rate.

A related problem is that if the student reads very slowly, it is hard for the student to look ahead and fit the next word into the sentence. Consider this sentence:

Before he   knew   what was happening,

Brad found himself   in the water.

The slow reader might well read "Before he" as a sentence, "what was happening" as a sentence, and "Brad found himself" as a sentence. Even if the clumping of the parts is not this extreme, the slow reader would have more trouble putting the pieces together to make a coherent sentence than the faster reader would. So a simple rule about rate is that if rate is sufficiently close to normal speaking rate, readers can listen to what they read nearly as easily as they can listen to others who say the same sentences.

Viewing the problem a different way, the learner has only so much attention. If the learner struggles to read the words faster and faster, the learner has limited leftover attention for comprehension. If the learner can read accurately at close to a normal rate and do so without great strain, the learner has more attention available for comprehending.

Note that this is only a potential. If learners are not reinforced for understanding what they read and for retaining the information, the question of reading rate is moot. Some learners may remain functionally illiterate at any rate.

Why Oral Fluency Practice?

The main purpose for making the practice oral is that it permits us to hear what the learner is reading. If we use silent reading, we don't have clear information about the learner's accuracy or rate.

What are the practical concerns with a slow oral-reading rate? The most obvious is that the slow-reading students will require longer to do work than the faster readers. Also, as noted above, the slow readers do not develop the strategy of looking ahead to identify the next word while saying the current word (just as one has to think ahead to formulate a sequence of words before saying them).

To demonstrate the effects of rate on comprehension, read the following sentences at the rate of about 30 words per minute.

That's two seconds per word. The passage is 30 words. So it should take you one minute to read it. As you read, think about what the learner is probably doing that requires so much time per word.

> Al and Hersten left for school at eight thirty. On their way, they saw Amy fall down in the street. Before they could help her, Dennis ran into the street.

1 The student who reads at a very slow rate is obviously concentrating on decoding each word. The rate is typical of students who are stalled at the stage of sounding out each word rather than visually recognizing the spelling of each word.

2 Because the learner devotes so much mental energy to decoding, there is little room left for comprehension. To comprehend, the learner would have to remember some of the words that were read nearly a minute earlier. This is probably impossible unless the learner keeps summarizing the passage to date or answers comprehension questions after reading each sentence. Without looking back at the passage again, answer these questions:

○ What were the names of the children going to school?

○ What was the name of the person who fell?

○ What was the name of the person who ran into the street?

These questions are far harder to answer when the information trickled in at a very low rate.

Read the following paragraph aloud, at a normal speaking rate. Then answer the questions:

> The article named Mr. Fredricks as the insider who worked as a bookkeeper and secretly photographed all of Jenkins'

correspondence. Mr. Fredricks and Judy moved to Australia shortly after testifying.

○ Who do you suppose was on trial?

○ Who testified?

○ What do you suppose Mr. Fredricks testified about?

Obviously the questions are much more difficult, but if you read the passage orally at a normal speaking rate, you understand it about as well as you would if somebody said it to you.

How Fast Is an Adequate Oral-Reading Rate?

Years ago, educators believed the myth that the faster readers read, the better they were in comprehending. Clearly, that can't be the case. Educators were confused because they observed a correlation between reading rate and comprehension, which was the result of the faster readers also being better comprehenders. However, this correlation did not suggest that poor readers would comprehend better if they simply rattled off words at a faster rate.

Some things must be read at a slow rate because they are complicated and require more processing time to extract meaning from them. If somebody started to orally present the same text at a very high rate, you would probably say, "Whoa. Could you start over and go more slowly? You lost me in the first sentence."

It is true that there is no problem working on rate that is not interrupted with comprehension issues so that students can focus on simply reading faster. The question is, how much of this type of reading should a student do? Although it is fine to eat spinach, a diet that consists primarily of spinach is probably not fine. Similarly, focusing on rate without comprehension puts priorities out of balance. Rate is not everything, and it is certainly not as important as either accuracy or comprehension.

Objectives

An effective rate-improvement program would meet the following objectives:

- The program must make it clear to the students that accuracy is the primary goal and rate improvement occurs within the framework of reading accurately. (Students are preempted from comprehending if they don't read accurately.)

- The goals or expectations for students improving are based solely on each individual child's performance (not on a schedule that indicates what rate is to be achieved by what date).

- The goals are reached in a scientific manner, with the practices governed by sound principles of reinforcement.

- The goals are based on evidence that the student will be able to achieve them.

- Students receive ongoing data to document their improvement.

A highly effective program for low performers meets all these criteria. Of necessity, this program is somewhat labor intensive. One reason is that the program must be individualized for each student and presented one-on-one. Another reason is that the teacher must collect data regularly and use it to adjust student expectations, to reinforce the student, and to diagnose whether the placement of the student is appropriate.

Time to Read 250 Words versus Words per Minute

The sequence for the *Differentiated Reinforcement Fluency* (DRF) program does not use the standard measure for rate—words per minute. Instead, DRF timings are based on **how long it takes the student to read a 250-word passage.** This may seem like an arbitrary practice, but it is not. DRF *B1* uses time to read 250 words primarily because this measure shows improvement for low performers far more dramatically than words per minute does. Although words per minute is a reasonable way of measuring fluency for students who read in the range of normal spoken conversations, it is not well designed for students who read very slowly. Specifically, very slow readers may achieve great gains in their reading rate, but if we measure their performance as words per minute, the achievement is not impressive.

Table 1 shows the relationship of time required to read 250 words and words per minute for a learner who initially reads at 40 words per minute. It takes the learner 6:15 minutes to read a 250-word passage. The learner improves until she reads a 250-word passage in 6 minutes. As the first column of the table shows, that is an improvement of 15 seconds to read the passage. When the same performance is expressed as words per minute (second column), the improvement is only 1 word per minute, from 40 WPM to 41 WPM. Improving by 15 seconds seems far more impressive than improving 1 word per minute.

Table 1

Time required to read 250-word passage	Words per Minute
6:15	40
6:12	40
6:09	40
6:06	41
6:03	41
6:00	41
Improvement	
15 seconds	**1** word

Not only is the improvement in time impressive to the student, it provides the teacher with clear evidence that the student is improving. In contrast, the teacher may not be impressed by an improvement of 1 word per minute.

As the learner reads faster than 41 words per minute, the gap between the time required to read a 250-word passage and words per minute narrows.

Table 2 shows the relationship between the measures when the learner improves from reading the passage in 3:50 to reading it in 3:35.

Table 2

Time required to read 250-word passage	Words per minute
3:50	65
3:47	66
3:44	67
3:41	68
3:38	68
3:35	69
Improvement	
15 seconds	**4** words

The improvement in time to read 250 words is still 15 seconds. The improvement in words per minute is 4 (from 65 WPM to 69 WPM). Although the difference is not as great as it is for the learner who initially reads at 40 words per minute, the improvement in time to read 250 words is still over three times the improvement in words per minute (15 seconds versus 4 words).

Crossover Point

When the learner reads a 250-word passage in 2:02, the measures are equal. The learner is now reading 122 words per minute, and the time required to read the passage is 122 seconds. For rates that are faster than 122 words per minute, the gains in words per minute are greater than corresponding improvements in time to read 250 words.

Table 3 shows how the crossover points change as the length of the passage changes. If the passage is 100 words, the crossover point is 77 words per minute. At this point,

the student reads the passage in 77 seconds at the rate of 77 words per minute.

Table 3
Crossover Points

Passage length	Time required to read passage	Words per minute
100	77 seconds (1:17)	77 WPM
200	110 seconds (1:50)	110 WPM
250	122 seconds (2:02)	122 WPM
300	134 seconds (2:14)	134 WPM

If the passage length is 200 words, the crossover point is 1:50, which is 110 seconds. At this time the student reads 110 words per minute.

If the passage is 300 words, the crossover point is 2:14, which is 134 seconds. The student reads at 134 words per minute.

If the student reads the passage at a rate slower than the crossover rate, the gain in time improvement expressed as time to read the passage is greater than the improvement in words per minute.

Note: DRF level B1 presents 250-word passages, and the crossover point is 122 words per minute. So students who read 40 words per minute will see great improvement if their reading rate increases 5 words per minute. (Their time to read the passage will improve from 6 minutes 15 seconds to 5 minutes 33 seconds—an improvement of 42 seconds.) Even if these students do not achieve a rate of more than 60 words per minute at the end of DRF level B1, the students will be confident and will have sound reasons to believe that their reading performance will continue to improve.

DRF Design

Reinforcement Strategies

The basic DRF strategy is designed to accelerate the performance of slow readers by giving them decoding practice with material they are able to read and by using a reinforcement system that is tailored to their specific performance level and that encourages them to improve in rate-accuracy, without putting them under pressure to reach objectives.

The reinforcement practices derive from these facts:

1 If you took a sample of six passages, each the same length and composed entirely of words the student knows, the student would not read them at the same rate. A couple would be above average, two would be around the same time, and typically two would be below the average time.

2 If students approach the task of learning to improve in reading rate-accuracy with a positive attitude (I'm getting better and better at reading), they will learn faster and more comfortably than they would if they approach the task with a more negative attitude (I am not doing well; I must do better). The negative orientation promotes anxiety, much superstitious behavior, and lots of self-corrects and guesses.

The formula for taking advantage of these facts is to put a stronger emphasis on success than on failure. Arrange the odds so that students will probably receive reinforcement for the next selection they read aloud. Arrange it so that even if learners do not improve on the selection read today, they will understand that they are reading adequately and that they'll probably perform better on the following selection.

The DRF program awards points for the student's performance. The design and schedule for awarding points take advantage of these facts. The schedule is biased so students receive 2 points if they perform better than their average and 1 point if they perform around their average. They receive no points for performing significantly below their average.

With this schedule, a student who does not improve over the performance on his earlier readings will receive some reinforcement on four of the six selections. Two of these readings will have "double reinforcement" (2 points), which is evidence of improvement, and only two readings will have no reinforcement. With the probabilities stacked this way, it is far easier for the learner to try to work for a higher rate of more "reinforcement readings." The learner who improves only slightly will receive more than 2 double reinforcements and either 1 or 0 no-reinforcement readings. The learner who improves more than a little may receive as many as 4 double reinforcements, 2 single reinforcements, and no readings that earn 0 points.

This plan is the essence of individualized instruction. Individual learners show the teacher through their behavior what they can do. The evidence is stacked so students will not fail; they will try hard to improve; they will feel good about their performance.

Differentiated Reinforcement Fluency for B1

As the discussion above indicates, the key feature of differentiated reinforcement is that it provides students with evidence of improvement in fluency and accuracy through techniques that encourage improvement, without referencing their performance to pre-established benchmarks. Instead, each student's goals are referenced to the student's current performance. The reinforcement schedule is designed so students earn points. Students who beat their current average time by a lot earn more points than students who don't beat their current performance by as much. In all cases, however, students will receive some points for performing at their current level. They will not have to work under the threat of failing to meet a benchmark. They simply won't receive as many points as they would if they performed a little better.

Six Reasons DRF Works Well

Understand that DRF works, even for students who have a history of frustration in trying to read faster with sufficient accuracy.[1] DRF succeeds for 6 reasons:

1 The students show through their behavior the maximum rate at which they can improve fluency performance. All gains are referenced to these changes in performance. The result is that students receive evidence that they are capable learners and that their reading skills are improving.

2 The program is designed so that the initial probability of a student earning either 1 point or 2 points on a timing is 4 out of 6. As the student improves, the schedule for reinforcements (points) changes so students typically earn points on 5 of 6 or 6 of 6 fluency timings.

3 The design of the point schedule encourages students to improve more rapidly by awarding 2 points for gains that are achievable but are greater than average performance (which earns 1 point).

4 The baseline for awarding points changes as a student improves, but the changes always occur so that even students who do not improve above their current average range of performance will receive 2 points on at least 3 of the 6 timings.

5 The program does not involve drills or repeated reading, simply a single reading of passages that do not tax the students' skills. The procedures show students that their goal is simply to obtain a higher percentage of timings that earn 2 points.

6 Equally important, the students' fluency rate is always evaluated within the context of accuracy. Students receive no reinforcement when they make more than 10 reading errors on a 250-word passage. The procedures, therefore, shape the students' strategies for reading faster within the context of correctly identifying each word.

1. See "Shaping the Response" (pp. 255–256) in Engelmann & Carnine (1991) Theory of Instruction. For description of techniques used with low performers (reading), see "Teaching Academic Skills to School-Age Children" (pp. 355–358). Note performance of children with IQs under 71, 71–90, and 91–100 in figure 30.3 (p.358).

Program Overview

General Description

Corrective Reading stories are well designed for rate-accuracy timings because they are composed completely of words that students are able to decode. Furthermore, the schedule for introducing DRF stories assures that students have already read each selection that is to be timed.

The B1 level of DRF is designed for students who have completed lesson 25 in *Corrective Reading* Decoding B1. The DRF sequence does not start earlier because the earlier work in *Corrective Reading* focuses primarily on accuracy, not fluency.

Level B1 of DRF provides 6 baseline timings and 45 fluency sessions. The selections read are drawn from *B1* lessons 15–65. All selections that students read for fluency practice have been read at least 10 school days earlier in the *Corrective Reading* sequence. (The first baseline blackline master, BL-A, is from *B1* lesson 15, BL-B is from lesson 16, and so forth.) Students should be able to read these selections more fluently than passages they had never read before.

The teacher uses a point-and-graphing system (pages 36–43) that shows students the number of points they earn for each timing. After baseline, students receive 1 point if they remain at baseline levels of rate and accuracy, and they receive 2 points if they perform better than their average performance. For performance that is below their average, they receive no points. As their rate improves, the teacher adjusts the performance requirement for achieving 1 point and 2 points.

After baseline, students do not earn points for a passage unless they read it making 10 or fewer errors. The error rate of 4 errors per 100 (10 per 250) words is far more liberal than we would expect the reader to make, but if we do not allow some latitude, students become very anxious trying to read accurately at a faster rate. The more liberal error criterion assures that students will be able to do some experimentation without being penalized. The 10-error limit assures that when students try to guess or employ any other "shortcut" strategy, they will receive information that the strategy is not effective.

Who Needs DRF Program Practice?

The B1 level DRF sequence is designed for students who initially read at a rate considerably slower than 60 words per minute (possibly as low as 40 words per minute). Students read 250-word passages and graph their results. The graph provides a realistic portrayal of their improvement.

The first question you should ask before placing any student in the DRF sequence is: **Are you sure that the student who needs fluency practice is able to read all the words in the sequence of selections you will present?** If a student cannot read *all the words* that will be presented in the first 6 selections without additional rehearsal, you must reteach the lessons in which these words were taught before proceeding with the DRF sequence.

The DRF is not recommended for higher performers who could learn to improve their rate-accuracy by simply doing paired reading with a partner. Even if the student who is monitoring the high-performing reader does not catch all the errors, paired practice will be effective for high-performing students. With low performers, however, a more careful approach is needed to assure that students receive the kind of practice that demonstrates to them that they are meeting rate-accuracy goals and are receiving a relatively high rate of reinforcement for their efforts.

Who Monitors the Reading?

Students read individually. Each reading is monitored. The student reads aloud to the monitor, who records time and errors. The monitor may be a peer, an older student, an aide, a parent volunteer, or a teacher.

Higher-performing students as monitors This is the best option if you have 6 or more students who need work on fluency. The higher-performing students need to be trained in the procedures and need to understand that they are providing an important service for the children they serve. With a brief orientation and some monitoring and reinforcement, higher performers do an excellent job of working with lower-performing children.

Parents, teachers, or aides as monitors The option of a parent, a teacher, or an aide is reasonable under the following conditions:

1. The monitors are available for every school day during the timing periods.
2. The classroom needs only one or possibly two monitors.

If there are six children who need fluency practice, a parent, teacher, or aide could be the most effective solution. In about 45 minutes, one person would be able to monitor the readings for all six children. **Note:** If this person is not available five days a week, it is possible to use two people; however, the schedule must be clear and the procedures must be the same for both monitors.

Peers as monitors Although the format of students working in pairs is generally not very successful for low performers who need fluency practice, peers may be the only option. Ideally, the peer doing the monitoring is a higher performer. The best procedure is to identify an A member and a B member of each pair and orchestrate the timings so that all pairs start reading at the same time, while you circulate among the pairs and confirm that the monitors are following procedures. Note that the plan requires significant amounts of your time. You will have to check after each reading to make sure the monitors are recording errors and the readers are graphing their performance correctly. If you do not assure that the monitors are performing adequately, scant positive results will come from the fluency work.

Daily Scheduling

Timings are to be done daily. If they are done less frequently, they are not as effective because the fluency passages that students read are less like the material they are reading during the daily reading periods. For example, if students do daily timings, they read one passage during a session. Students have read the passage 10 lessons earlier. If students do timings only three times a week for four weeks, the passage timed will have been presented 18 lessons earlier, which means it is a bit more elementary than the selections students are currently reading in their reading periods.

Allocate about 8 minutes for each student to complete the reading of the selections and recording of the data. (If students work in pairs, each student is timed, so the total time required for the pair would be about 16 minutes. If monitors are in the classroom for 25 minutes, each can do timing sessions for three children (depending on fluency of the readers). With five older students, the timings for 15 students could be completed in about 25 minutes.

The most important scheduling detail is that **the DRF program should not occur during the period specified for teacher-directed reading.** The time scheduled for the daily reading period is absolutely necessary for at-risk children, and no part of it should be sacrificed for timings. It may be possible to schedule the timings during an "independent work" period that is actually part of the reading period but is not the part that is teacher-directed.

The qualification for doing timings during an independent-work period is that the timings must be orchestrated in a way that does not require much more than 8 minutes for each student to do the timing and record the results. The 8-minute interruption would still allow students to complete the independent work. If it turns out that students are not able to complete their work, another time should be used for DRF.

Materials

The DRF materials include:

- blackline masters of the selections students read.

- blackline masters of the forms used to record data on each timing.

- blackline masters of graphs students use to plot their progress.

Selections

The materials for the timings appear in Part 3, beginning on page 36.

Table 4 shows the DRF schedule for presenting the selections.

Column 1 of the schedule shows *B1* lessons. The fluency practice for *B1* begins after lesson 25. Column 2 shows the selections for each DRF session. The selections that are read for baseline are numbered BL-A through BL-F. The post-baseline selections are numbered 1 through 45. Column 3 shows the *B1* lessons from which selections were drawn. Note that 10 of the timings would be scheduled after students have completed the last lesson in *B1* (lesson 65). These timings could be presented at the rate of three or four a day or during the first part of *B2*.

Table 4: DRF B1 Schedule

	1	2	3
	Begin after B1 Lesson	**DRF Session**	**Story drawn from B1 Lesson**
Baseline	25	BL-A	15
	26	BL-B	16
	27	BL-C	17
	28	BL-D	18
	29	BL-E	19
	30	BL-F	20
Post-Baseline	31	1	21
	32	2	22
	33	3	23
	34	4	24
	35	5	25
	36	6	26
	37	7	27
	38	8	28
	39	9	29
	40	10	30
	41	11	31
	42	12	32
	43	13	33
	44	14	34
	45	15	35
	46	16	36
	47	17	37
	48	18	38
	49	19	39
	50	20	40
	51	21	41
	52	22	42
	53	23	43
	54	24	44
	55	25	45
	56	26	46
	57	27	47
	58	28	48
	59	29	49
	60	30	50
	61	31	51
	62	32	52
	63	33	53
	64	34	54
	65	35	55
		36	56
		37	57
		38	58
		39	59
		40	60
		41	61
		42	62
		43	63
		44	64
		45	65

Reproducible Stories

The blackline masters of the stories appear in Part 3 of this guide, starting on page 44. At the bottom of each selection is an indication of the *B1* lesson that is to immediately precede that selection.

Here is the blackline master page for post-baseline session 24.

This is the material for the twenty-fourth timing session after baseline. The selection is to be presented on the same day the reading group completes *B1* lesson 54. The passage is from lesson 44.

STORY 24

Henry was trying to fix his motor, but he was not doing very	13
well. He was looking at the words in his book on motors, but	26
Henry did not know what they said. The book said: "To turn a	39
cam shaft, you file each cam."	45
But this is what Henry said as he was reading: "To turn a	58
cam shaft, you fill each cam."	64
Henry said, "What does that mean?" He tossed the book	74
aside and said, "That book is not helping me very much. I can	87
do the job myself." So Henry worked and worked.	96
After a while, his motor was in little bits. Now he did not	109
have a motor. He had a heap of steel.	118
"Where is the cam shaft?" he asked as he looked at the big	131
pile of steel.	134
He picked up a big gear. "Is this a cam shaft?" he asked. He	148
ran his hand over the teeth of the gear. "These things must be	161
the cams," he said.	165
Henry was looking at the gear when a truck came down the	177
street. The truck was dragging his sister's hot rod.	186
Molly was mad. She ran over to Henry and said, "Where is	198
that book? My motor broke down, and I've got to fix it fast."	211
Molly grabbed the book. She ran to her hot rod and began	223
to work.	225
When it was time for dinner, Molly had fixed her hot rod.	237
She had taken the pan and taken three bent rods from the motor. ★	250

Story above follows Lesson 54

B1 Decoding   73

Calculating Words per Minute

The numbers in the right margin provide a running total of words for the selection. If the school district requires reports based on words per minute, make a slash mark on your copy of the selection to show the last word the student read after one minute has elapsed. The student continues to read to the end of the selection. If the slash mark is in the middle of a line, subtract the number of unread words on the line from the number in the margin.

If reports call for reporting *correct* words per minute in addition to total words, count the errors that occur before the slash mark and subtract them from total words read.

Procedures

Presenting Timings During Baseline

Introducing the Timings to the Students

Introduce the timings before presenting the first baseline session. Part 2 of this guide, page 26, includes a script for presenting this introduction (Script 1—*Introducing Baseline Timings*). The introduction should not take more than about 3 minutes.

Administering the Baseline Timings

The monitor will use the following procedures to direct the reading and to record data. Note that a variation of the procedure is used throughout the program.

The student reads from one copy of the selection. The monitor marks errors on a second copy. Note that each timing requires two copies of the selection.

1. The monitor places the selection facedown in front of the student (so the student is not able to "rehearse" it before the timing).

2. The monitor then tells the student, "Turn the paper over and touch the first word."

3. As soon as the student touches the first word, the monitor says, "Start reading," and simultaneously starts the timer (or records the starting time).

4. The monitor marks all mistakes on the monitor's copy of the passage. Mistakes include words that are misread, words that are skipped, and words the learner is not able to read within about 2 seconds.

5. If the student gets stuck on a word for 2 seconds, the monitor tells the student the word and tells the student to keep reading. There are no correction procedures during the timed readings because they would greatly distort the reading-fluency rate. The rate is also distorted if the student takes more than 2 seconds to figure out a word.

6. The timing continues until the student has read the word that is followed by a star. **The monitor records the time at this word, but the student continues reading until the end of the passage.**

Response to Errors

During baseline, the monitor marks all errors (from the beginning to the star) on the monitor's copy of the passage. **The monitor does not correct words.**

1. For words that the student omitted or misread, the monitor underlines the word or words involved in the error. If the student omits 2 words, the monitor underlines those words without interrupting the student. Each word that is underlined is counted as 1 error.

2. For words that are added, the monitor makes a caret (^) where the word is inserted. Each caret is counted as 1 error.

3. If the student skips a line or starts to reread a line, the monitor touches where the student should be reading, says, "Start here," and makes a caret at the beginning of the line in which the error occurred. Each caret counts as 1 error.

After the student completes the selection,

a. the monitor tells the student the time for reading the selection.

b. the monitor tells the student the number of errors the student made.

c. the monitor points to each underlined word and asks, "What is this word?" If the student does not answer correctly within 2 seconds, the monitor tells the word, then retests that word after testing the other words.

Recording Data During Baseline

The first 6 timings provide baseline information about the learner's performance. You establish a baseline of each student's rate-accuracy performance on these 6 passages (BL-A through BL-F) **before you start working on rate improvement.** The goal of baseline is to disclose the student's average reading rate and accuracy so that you have reasonable expectations for improving the student's performance. Baseline procedures are designed to put students at ease, in a setting that does not place unreasonable demands on them and that provides positive reinforcement.

Below is part of the form from page 36.

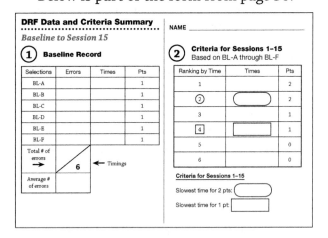

The monitor uses this part to record information for the 6 baseline timings. The Baseline Record shows the DRF selection, the number of errors the student made, the time the student required to read 250 words, and the points the student earned.

Selections The first column lists the 6 baseline selections.

Errors After the student has completed each passage, the monitor counts the number of decoding errors (each underlined word and each caret) and enters the total number in the Errors column. If the student makes 7 errors on selection BL-A, the monitor enters 7 in the Errors column.

After the student has read all 6 baseline selections, the monitor totals the errors and writes the total as the numerator of the fraction below the errors for BL-F. In Example 1, the student made a total number of 36 errors on the 6 selections. The monitor enters the number 36, creating the fraction $^{36}/_{6}$. Finally the monitor computes the average number of errors by dividing 36 by 6, which is 6.)

Times The monitor records the amount of time the student took to read the passage in the Times column.

Points During baseline, all students receive 1 point for reading each selection, regardless of the time or number of errors. (After baseline, the monitor will award 0, 1, or 2 points for each selection, based on the reader's baseline performance.)

Here is a filled-out Baseline Record form.

EXAMPLE 1

① Baseline Record

Selections	Errors	Times	Pts
BL-A	7	5:46	1
BL-B	11	5:25	1
BL-C	8	5:22	1
BL-D	3	5:50	1
BL-E	4	6:15	1
BL-F	3	5:30	1
Total # of errors →	36 / 6	← Timings	
Average # of errors	6		

The number of errors for the 6 baseline readings varies from 3 to 11. The total errors is 36. The average number of errors is 6. The times range from 5:22 to 6:15.

Placing the Student

To qualify for the DRF program sequence, students have to meet two criteria, one for accuracy and one for rate. Students do not qualify for the DRF program if they fail either the accuracy criterion or the rate criterion. These students need to be placed in material easy enough for them to meet both criteria. They also benefit from duet reading. (See page 22.)

Accuracy criterion Students who average fewer than 11 errors qualify for DRF. Students who make an average of 11 or more errors do not qualify for DRF. They need practice in reading accurately before they begin working on fluency.

Rate criterion Students who exceed 7 minutes (35 WPM) on 3 or more of the baseline timings do not qualify for the DRF program.

The filled-out baseline form for Example 1, above, shows that the student met the accuracy criterion. The student made fewer than 11 errors on all but one of the DRF selections (BL-B). The student's average number of errors was 6—well below the error limit of 10.

The student also met the rate criterion, performing well within the 7-minute criterion on all selections.

Here is the performance of a student who does not qualify for the DRF program.

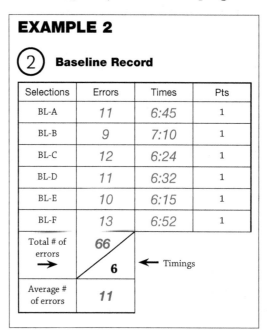

EXAMPLE 2

② Baseline Record

Selections	Errors	Times	Pts
BL-A	11	6:45	1
BL-B	9	7:10	1
BL-C	12	6:24	1
BL-D	11	6:32	1
BL-E	10	6:15	1
BL-F	13	6:52	1
Total # of errors →	66 / 6	← Timings	
Average # of errors	11		

Accuracy criterion The student failed the accuracy criterion. The Errors column shows that the student made 11 or more errors on four selections. The total number of errors is 66, which yields an average score of 11 errors per selection.

Points during baseline As noted above, the monitor awards students 1 point for every timing during baseline, regardless of the time or number of mistakes the student makes. The monitor tells students they did a good job and tried hard (unless they obviously were not trying hard). The purpose of this procedure is to assure that students make an effort during baseline. If they receive no reinforcement for the timings, at least some of them will conclude that a timing is just an activity that must be performed. We want learners to try hard during baseline so their performance will provide a good measure of how well they read.

Establishing a Point Schedule for the Next 15 Sessions

At the end of the sixth timing, you identify those students who are appropriately placed in DRF. For those who qualify, **you first establish their schedule for earning points for the next 15 timings.** Note: The schedule is not the same for different students. The schedule is based strictly on each student's rate-accuracy baseline performance.

The post-baseline procedures are different from those used during baseline in two ways:

■ Following baseline, students do not automatically receive 1 point for each timing. Students may earn 2 points, 1 point, or no points for each timing, depending on their time.

■ Following baseline, students stay on a point schedule for 15 sessions (rather than 6). Following every fifteenth lesson, the point schedule is updated.

Ranking the selections according to time For students who meet the rate-accuracy criteria, the monitor ranks the 6 baseline times from the fastest time to the slowest time.

Below are the times for Example 1. The table on the right shows the times rearranged from fastest to slowest. The fastest time is 5:22; the slowest 6:15.

Example 1

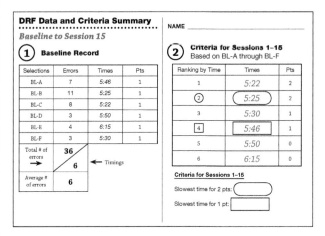

The timing shown in the oval (5:25) is the slowest time that will earn 2 points. The timing shown in the box (5:46) is the slowest time that earns 1 point. Any times slower than 5:46 receive no points. Here is the table with the point information shown in blue.

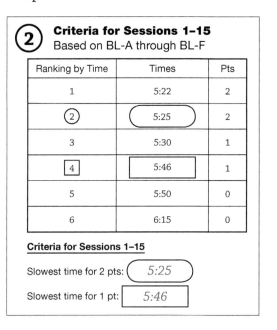

2 Criteria for Sessions 1–15
Based on BL-A through BL-F

Ranking by Time	Times	Pts
1	5:22	2
②	5:25	2
3	5:30	1
4	5:46	1
5	5:50	0
6	6:15	0

Criteria for Sessions 1–15

Slowest time for 2 pts: 5:25

Slowest time for 1 pt: 5:46

To calculate the point schedule for each student who qualifies for DRF, follow these steps:

1. Rank each student's 6 baseline times from fastest to slowest.
2. Designate time 2 as the slowest time that earns 2 points.
3. Designate time 4 as the slowest time that earns 1 point.

Post-Baseline Procedures

Here is the order of events during sessions that follow baseline:

1. Students read the selection first and the monitor records the data (time, errors, points).
2. Students graph the points for the timing. If the timing earned 2 points, the student graphs 2 points. If the timing earned 1 point, the student graphs 1 point. If the timing earned no points, the student graphs a line that goes straight across.

The procedures monitors follow for post-baseline sessions are different from the baseline procedures because students do not receive any points for a selection if they go over the error limit of 10.

During the reading, the monitor marks all errors on the monitor's copy of the passage.

1. For words that are omitted or misread, the monitor underlines the word or words involved in the error. If the student omits 2 words, the monitor underlines those words without interrupting the student. Each word that is underlined is counted as 1 error.
2. For words that are added, the monitor makes a caret (^) where the word is inserted. Each caret is counted as 1 error.
3. If the student skips a line or starts to reread a line, the monitor touches where the student should be reading, says, "Start here," and makes a caret at the beginning of the line in which the error occurred. Each caret counts as 1 error.

Note:

▪ **The monitor does not correct words.**

▪ **The monitor circles the eleventh error** (but permits the student to read to the end of the selection) and then tells the student, "The timing doesn't count because you made more than 10 errors."

After the reading, the monitor tells the student how the timing went.

1. The monitor tells the student the time for reading the selection.
2. The monitor tells the student the number of errors the student made.
3. The monitor points to each underlined word and asks, "What is this word?" If the student does not answer correctly within 2 seconds, the monitor tells the word, then retests that word after testing the other words.

Graphing Points

> Reproducible graphs are available in Part 3 (pages 36–43). Post-baseline presentation script (Script 2) begins on page 27.

After reading the selection, students graph points for their time. The goal of graphing is to provide students with evidence that they are improving and hopefully that they are performing better than they did during baseline. Presentation Script 2 (pages 27–34) details these procedures. The goal is for students to graph their performance, but for very low students, the monitor will have to draw lines on the graph.

Use Script 2 (pages 27–34) to introduce these procedures immediately after students read selection BL-F and before students do session 1.

The rate the line ascends on the graph depends on the number of points the student earns for a session. If the student's performance for a session earns 2 points, the line that is graphed ascends two places. If the student earns 1 point, the line ascends one place. If the student's reading does not earn any points, the line does not ascend.

The connected dots in the practice graph show that the student has completed three sessions. The student earned 2 points for session 1, 1 point for session 2, and 2 points for session 3.

The dots show the three possibilities for session 4: The lowest dot indicates where the line goes if the student earns no points; the middle dot shows 1 point; the highest dot shows 2 points.

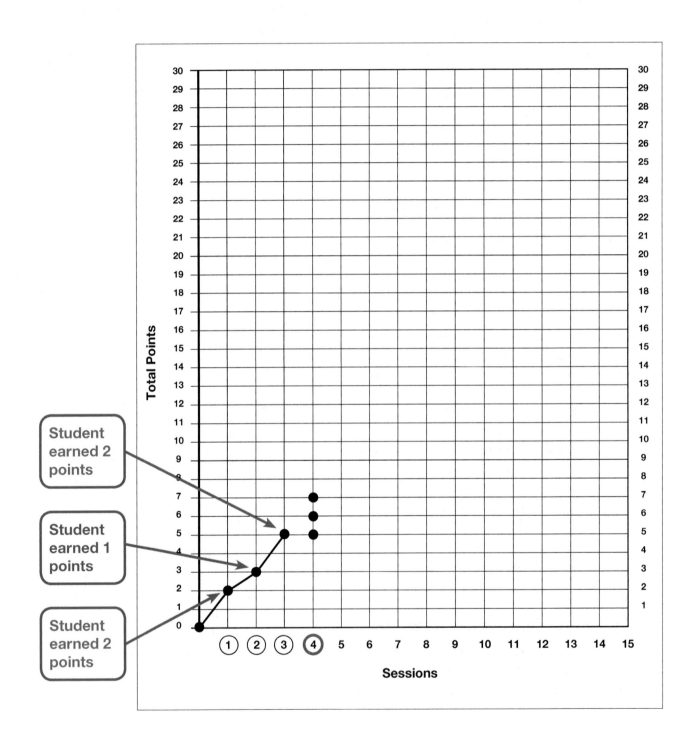

Student earned 2 points

Student earned 1 points

Student earned 2 points

Changes in Point Schedules

You update the schedule for awarding points after every 15 sessions using the following procedures.

1 Arrange the **last 6 timings** from fastest to slowest. (**Note:** These 6 timings come from the six sessions immediately before the schedule is updated. The first update occurs after session 15, so the 6 timings that are ranked come from sessions 10–15.)

2 Write the time for the second fastest timing (which is in an oval) in the oval for **slowest time for 2 points.**

3 Write the time for the fourth fastest timing (which is in a box) in the box for **slowest time for 1 point.**

In the examples that follow, a student's most recent 6 scores are arranged from fastest to slowest.

EXAMPLE 3

A completed schedule is shown below.

4 Criteria for Sessions 16–30
Based on 10 through 15

Ranking by Time	Times	Pts
1	4:57	2
②	5:10	2
3	5:21	1
4	5:39	1
5	5:40	0
6	5:57	0

Criteria for Sessions 1–15

Slowest time for 2 pts: 5:10

Slowest time for 1 pt: 5:39

EXAMPLE 4

The process is repeated after the next 15 sessions. Example 4 shows the most recent 6 scores arranged in order.

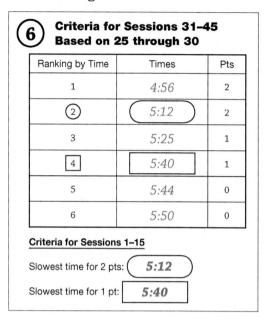

6 Criteria for Sessions 31–45
Based on 25 through 30

Ranking by Time	Times	Pts
1	4:56	2
②	5:12	2
3	5:25	1
4	5:40	1
5	5:44	0
6	5:50	0

Criteria for Sessions 1–15

Slowest time for 2 pts: 5:12

Slowest time for 1 pt: 5:40

The reader's times are not as good as they were in the previous ten lessons (Example 3). The new criterion for earning 2 points is 5:12. That is slower than the previous criterion for 2 points (5:10). This apparent regression sometimes occurs. It is often interpreted to mean that the learner is regressing. Probably not. More probably, the material is harder.

Regardless of the reason, the learner has shown us how long it takes him to read the current materials we are presenting. If we stay true to the procedures, in time the learner's behavior will tend to have fewer regressions and provide a more stable pattern of improvement.

Note: After children complete lesson 65 of *Decoding B1,* you may continue the DRF sequence by presenting selections for sessions 36–45 in sequence. These timings could be presented at the rate of up to four stories a day. Follow the same procedures for awarding points you use after baseline.

Working with Lower Performers

Duet Reading

In addition to timed reading, slow readers benefit greatly from *duet reading*. Duet reading is not timed. Duet reading benefits students who are too low to qualify for the DRF program. Students must be able to accurately read all the duet-reading selections. If the students are at or beyond lesson 25 in *B1*, you may use DRF selections as the basis for duet reading. You may also use any other selections that students are able to decode without making more than about 5 errors per 100 words (12 errors per 250 words).

For duet reading, you and the student sit side by side, looking at the same copy of what is to be read. You point to all words. You and the student take turns reading words. For the first round, you read the first word, the student reads the next word, you read the next word, and so forth.

This technique is like magic for very slow readers, particularly those who have various kinds of superstitious reading behaviors, such as pausing a second or more before saying the word, touching under the word several times before reading it, frequently correcting themselves, or looking at you after every word to see if you approve of the response.

Note that you should not have two low performers doing duet reading with each other. There are far too many requirements for the lead partner directing the reading—being able to read accurately and fast, being able to point to words with proper timing, and being able to identify and correct mistakes. Note, however, that other students may serve as the director of duet reading with low performers. The directors need training in procedures and observations to make sure they are following the procedures.

The main reason duet reading is so effective is that it completely removes the context in which the student has been reading connected sentences and presents a task that is more like reading isolated words than reading connected text. The task is easier than reading isolated words, however, because there are context cues and a great deal of modeling words that the student will later read. For example, if the word **cat** appears in the first sentence, and it is your word to read, the student receives a model of reading that word correctly. When it appears again as the student's word, the student is less likely to wonder what the word is or worry about reading it correctly. Also, duet reading is designed so the student is looking ahead while you are reading a word. This is a behavior that the student must learn in order to read fluently.

Procedure You point to each word—those that you read and those the student reads. Timing is very important. Your timing sets the stage for how fast students will read. If you point to your word and pause a second or two before reading it, learners will tend to pause a second or two before reading the next word. If your timing is faster for your words, learners will tend to read their words with less latency. But you have to be careful not to give learners the impression that you are hurrying them.

The best way to do duet reading is to touch under each word you read and say the word in less than one second. Then quickly touch under the student's word and do not move your finger until the learner reads the word (or until about three seconds have passed).

As soon as the learner correctly identifies the word, move your finger under the next word, pause less than one second, and read the word.

To repeat: Do not pause more than an instant before reading *your* words. Do not adjust your pace to the student's pace. As soon as the student's word is read, touch under the next word. Do not hurry the student or show impatience. Simply model the procedure of touching under the word and reading the word quickly. Praise the student for improvement, which you and the student will probably notice immediately.

To correct mistakes Say, "No, that word is _____. What word?" Then say, "Let's do that part again." Go back four words, touch under the word, and read it. Then quickly touch under the next word. Do not sound out the word or require the student to repeat it.

Stop at the end of the next sentence, and praise the student for good reading.

The purpose of this procedure is to keep it low-key. Often low performers become uncertain and agitated. The simplest procedure for putting the student at ease is to show it is no big deal and you have no expectations that the student will read with perfect accuracy. You'll help the student with a low-key correction.

After reading an entire selection in this manner, reread it with the student reading the first word and you reading the next, and so forth. At the end of the second reading, the student would have read all the words in the selection.

After doing ten or more duet-reading sessions in which you point, change the format so the student points. At first, this may be a difficult task for the student. A good procedure is to do it only on the second reading and don't do it for the entire selection. Tell the student ahead of time, "You will do the pointing for part of this reading." Stop in the middle of the selection and tell the student, "You do it. Point to all the words. I'll read the first one, and you'll read the next one."

If a student has great difficulty, you could read all the words of the story as the student points. Vary the pace from sentence to sentence, so the student has to listen to what you are reading, rather than just move along each line of text at a fixed rate. You may also hold the learner's wrist and assist in the pointing and stopping.

Note that this format helps the learner treat words as units. The learner has to look for the next word, read or listen to the word being read, and anticipate the next word.

Variations After the student is fairly reliable about reading and pointing, you can make variations that shape fluency.

Introduce a multiple-word variation. The director reads the first two words, the learner reads the next two words, and so forth. For this variation, you do all the pointing. At first it's difficult for the learner to say the right number of words at the right time. You can prompt who is reading by using one finger to point to your words and two fingers to point to the learner's words. Point out that this kind of reading is very hard. The simplest format is for you to read two words and the student to read the next two. (It's simpler because the pattern is the same: two for you, two for the student.)

Next, you could change the procedure so you read one word and the student reads three. After 4 to 8 sessions in which the student reads words accurately at the rate of around 50 words a minute or more, drop the duet reading.

Interfacing Duet Reading with Timed Reading

The duet reading works with a full range of slower readers; however, it is most efficiently used with students who initially read very slowly—initially in the range of 40 to 60 words per minute.

The duet reading precedes the timings. The simplest procedure is to do 12 or fewer duet sessions with the student and then start the timings. The judgment about when to terminate the duet reading is based on student performance. When the student is both noticeably faster and accurate on three consecutive duet sessions, start the timings. Also, if a student is initially identified as one who does not need duet reading but performs poorly on the first two or three timings, either by making too many mistakes or having very slow times (over 6:15 for 250 words, about the rate of 40 words per minute), drop the timing and institute the duet reading.

Using DRF Practice with Other Sequenced Material

The procedures you use in the DRF program may be extended to other sequenced material. However, do *not* use DRF procedures with material that does not have a controlled vocabulary and "decodable text." What that means is that the practices are not appropriate for anthologies or material that contains words children do not know if the words are presented in isolation.

The material that is read for the extension of DRF practices should be read without timing 10 or more school days before students read it as a timed selection.

If children complete the DRF sequence earlier in the school year, you may choose to continue the fluency work until the end of the term.

You may continue the DRF sequence by using the Supplemental DRF Data and Criteria Summary form that appears in Part 3 on page 38 and the Supplemental Graph for Fluency Points that appears on page 43. The generic, supplemental forms have blanks in which you simply write the number of DRF sessions and follow the same procedures you used for post-baseline DRF sessions 1–45.

SRA **Differentiated Reinforcement Fluency**

Decoding B1

PART 2: Scripts

- **Script 1**—Introducing Baseline Timings

- **Script 2**—Introducing Post-Baseline Timings

PART 2: Scripts

SCRIPT 1—INTRODUCING BASELINE TIMINGS

Before presenting the first baseline timing, plan to spend about 5 minutes introducing the timings. You will need a copy of story BL-A and a copy of the first data form (page 36).

Here is a presentation script.

1. This program will improve your reading. You're going to read out loud to someone who will help you. If you read pretty well, you can earn points every time you read.

   • Every day you will read passages that are 250 words long. How long are the passages? (Signal.) *250 words.*

2. The person you read to will time how long it takes for you to read the passages. You are not to hurry or read faster than you can go without guessing.

   • Are you going to guess at words? (Signal.) *No.*

   • Are you going to try to read superfast? (Signal.) *No.*

3. You will try to read each word correctly. If you get stuck, the person you read to will help you out. You will earn 1 point for each story you read. Later, you will be able to earn as many as 2 points.

4. (Hold up the first data form, page 36.)

   • (Teacher reference:)

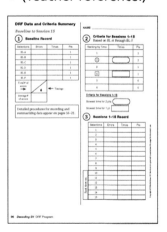

• We will keep records of the time it takes you to read each passage. Your reading will improve, and the record we keep will show how much your reading improves.

5. (Hold up the first selection, BL-A.)

   • (Teacher reference:)

• All the stories you will read are stories you've read before. This one is from lesson 15. This is the first story you will read. Next time, you'll read the story from 16.

• What's the first story you'll read? (Signal.) *15.*

6. The story for your reading group today is 25. You'll read that story again a few weeks from now. So when you work in your reading group, read carefully so you will be sure you know all the words in the stories you will read later.

END OF SCRIPT 1

Training Monitors for Baseline Timings

- Train monitors before they work with children.
- Make sure they know how to use a timer or the clock to measure time required to read the passage.
- Make sure they know how to record decoding mistakes.
  - carets for each added word or line skipped
  - underlines for each word that is omitted or misread
- Also, rehearse monitors in translating the data summaries to students.
- Make sure that monitors know the wording they will use to
  - help students when they get stuck.
  - inform students of the number of errors they made.
  - review words students missed (all carets and underlinings).

Before baseline, train monitors in the procedures that are specified on page 15. Rehearse with you playing the part of the reader. Present examples of you taking too long to read the word, skipping lines, rereading the same line, inserting words, omitting words, saying the wrong word. Do not read faster than about 40 words a minute during training.

After you read the selection, the monitors are to record the number of errors and the time. Then they are to tell you how many errors you made and your time for reading the passage.

Finally, the monitors are to point to each word you missed and direct you to read the word (saying the word if you do not respond in about 2 seconds).

SCRIPT 2—INTRODUCING POST-BASELINE TIMINGS

After students have completed baseline, establish a schedule for each student to earn 0, 1, or 2 points.

Present an orientation that introduces the procedures that will be used during all of the subsequent sessions. You will need a copy of the Practice Graph, page 39, for each student.

Present the following script:

1. You're going to do a timing every day. The more you improve, the more points you will earn. We will keep records that show how much you improve as you practice.

2. (Point to the circled ③ on the data form below:) You can see **1** through **15** on the record form.

- (Touch **1** and say:) **One.** That's where we will write the time for the first story you read.

- (Touch **15** and say:) **Fifteen.** That's where we will write the time for the fifteenth story you read.

(Script continues on next page.)

DRF Data and Criteria Summary

Baseline to Session 15

NAME _____

① Baseline Record

Selections	Errors	Times	Pts
BL-A			1
BL-B			1
BL-C			1
BL-D			1
BL-E			1
BL-F			1
Total # of errors →	6 ← Timings		
Average # of errors			

Detailed procedures for recording and summarizing data appear on pages 16–21.

② Criteria for Sessions 1–15
Based on BL-A through BL-F

Ranking by Time	Times	Pts
1		2
②	⬭	2
3		1
4	☐	1
5		0
6		0

Criteria for Sessions 1–15

Slowest time for 2 pts: ⬭

Slowest time for 1 pt: ☐

③ Sessions 1–15 Record

Selections	Errors	Times	Pts
1			
2			
3			
4			
5			
6			
7			
8			
9			
10			
11			
12			
13			
14			
15			

Rank these six.

36 *Decoding B1* DRF Program

28 *Decoding B1* DRF Program

(Script continues on next page.)

3. You earned 1 point for each story you have read. That means you have worked hard. From now on, you will have a chance to earn 2 points for each story you read very well.

- If you read very well, how many points can you earn? **(Signal.)** *Two.*

- You will earn 1 point if you read as well as you've been reading. But you will get no points if you read too slowly or make more than 10 errors.

- Can you earn points if you make 11 errors or more? **(Signal.)** *No.*

- Can you earn points if you make 10 errors? **(Signal.)** *Yes.*

- Can you earn points if you make 5 errors? **(Signal.)** *Yes.*

- Remember, if you read carefully, you can earn points. If you earn 1 point for every story, you are making some improvement. If you earn 2 points on a few stories, you're making a lot of improvement. If you earn 2 points on **most** of the stories you read, your improvement is amazing, but that should be your goal—to see how many selections you can read well enough to get 2 points.

4. From now on, you'll make a line to show how much you are improving.

5. (Show Graph 1, below:) Here's a graph that shows 1 point for every reading. That student is improving a lot.

- Watch. (Point to the circled ⑭, then move up to the heavy line:) In 14 readings, this student earned **14 points.**

- Watch. (Point to the circled ⑮ and move up the line:) How many points did the student earn in 15 readings? (Signal.) *15.*

(Script continues on next page.)

GRAPH 1

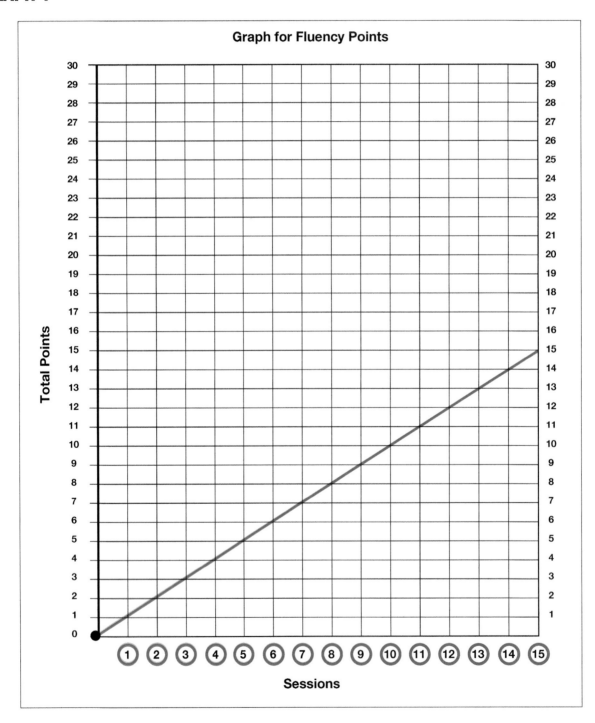

6. (Show Graph 2:) Here's a graph that shows a student who is improving, but not as much as the other student. On some days, this student earned zero points. On a few days, this student earned 1 point.

- (Point to A:) On this day, the student earned 1 point.

- (Point to B:) How many points did the student earn on this day? (Signal.) *Zero.*

- Yes, the student earned zero points.

- The first student earned 14 points after 14 days. Watch. (Touch the circled ⑭ on graph below and move up to the heavy line:) This student earned 3 points after 14 days.

- (Touch the circled ⑮ :) How many points did the student earn after 15 days? (Signal.) *Three.*

- Yes, only 3 points. That's not bad, but I think that student could have done better.

(Script continues on next page.)

GRAPH 2

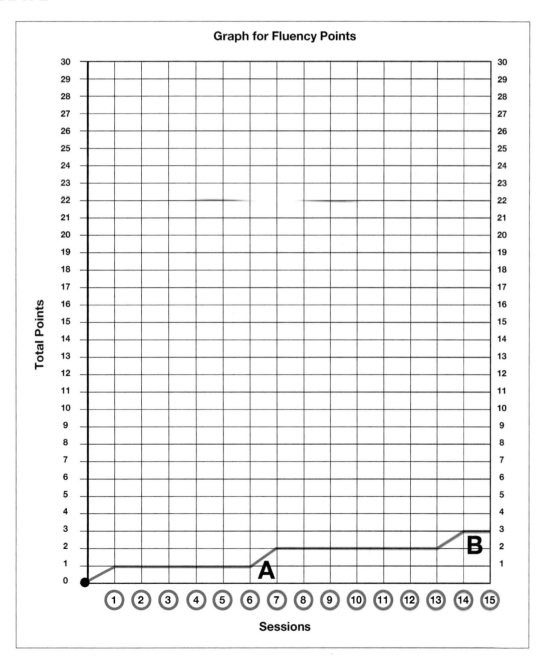

7. (Show Graph 3:) Here's a graph that shows 2 points for some days and 1 point for other days. This student's improvement is amazing. There are no days with a zero. On most of the days, the student earned 2 points.

- (Point to A:) On this day the student earned 2 points.

- (Point to B:) On this day, the student earned 1 point.

- (Point to C:) For 4 days in a row, this student earned 2 points. That's very impressive.

- Watch. (Point to the circled ⑭ and move up to the heavy line:) After 14 days, the student earned 21 points.

- Watch. (Point to the circled ⑮ and move up to the heavy line:) How many points did the student earn after 15 days? (Signal.) *23.*

- Yes, 23 points.

- Remember, your goal is to keep working until your graph looks like this one. And you can do it.

(Script continues on next page.)

GRAPH 3

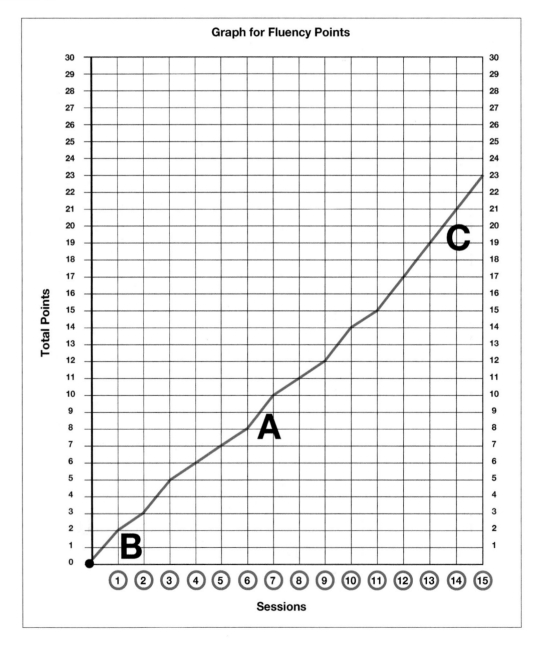

8. (Give each student one copy of the following Practice Graph that appears on page 39.)

- (Teacher reference:)

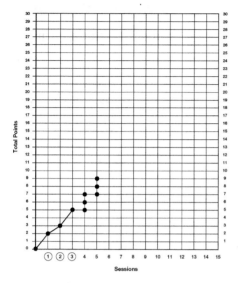

- After you have read the story, you will make a line on your graph to show how many points you earned that day. Part of the line on this student's graph has already been drawn. That line shows the points the student earned for stories 1, 2, and 3. You're going to draw the lines for stories 4 and 5. Touch the 4 at the bottom of the graph. √

- The first thing you do is circle the session number with your pencil. You're going to make a line for session 4, so circle 4. √

9. Go up the line for 4 to the three dots. √

- One of these dots shows where the line would go if the student earned 2 points. That's the top dot. Touch that dot.
(Observe students and give feedback.)

- One dot shows where the line would go if the student earned 1 point. That's the middle dot. Touch that dot.
(Observe students and give feedback.)

- One dot shows where the line would go if the student earned no points. Touch that dot.
(Observe students and give feedback.)

- Let's say you earned 2 points for session 4. Touch the dot for 2 points.
(Observe students and give feedback.)

10. Now touch the dot above 3.
(Observe students and give feedback.)

- Draw the line from the dot for 3 to the top dot for 4.
(Observe students and give feedback.)

- (Draw on board:)

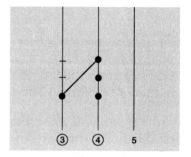

- Here's what you should have. Check your line. √

- That line went up 2 points. How many places did that line go up? (Signal.) Two.

- Yes, 2 points.

11. Now you're going to draw a line for session 5. Circle 5 at the bottom of the page. √

- Touch the top dot above 5.
(Observe students and give feedback.)

- That's the dot for 2 points. Touch the middle dot.
(Observe students and give feedback.)

- That's the dot for 1 point. Touch the dot for no points.
(Observe students and give feedback.)

- Draw the line from the dot for 4 to show that the student earned 1 point for 5. That's the middle dot.
  (Observe students and give feedback.)

- (Draw to show:)

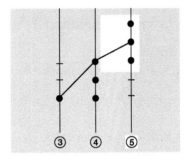

③   ④   ⑤

- Here's what you should have. Check your line. √

12. Your monitor will make the three dots for you on your graph each day. If you earn 2 points, will you draw the line to the top dot or the middle dot? (Signal.) *The top dot.*

- If you earn 1 point, will you draw the line to the middle dot or the bottom dot? (Signal.) *The middle dot.*

END OF SCRIPT 2

Training Monitors for Post-Baseline Timings

The only differences between the post-baseline procedures and those the monitors already know how to perform are

1. procedures when error limit is exceeded.

2. procedures for directing students to plot points earned for the timing.

When Error Limit (10) Is Exceeded

As soon as the student makes more than 10 errors, the monitor circles the eleventh error but permits the student to read to the end of the selection.

After timings in which students went over the error limit,

    a. the monitor shows the student the eleventh error and tells the student the

timing doesn't count because the student made more than 10 errors.

    b. the monitor follows the same word review procedure used for students who read the passage within the error limit.

- The monitor points to each underlined word and asks, "What is this word?"

- If the student does not answer correctly within 2 seconds, the monitor tells the word, then retests that word after testing the other words.

Directing Students to Plot Points Earned

Immediately after presenting review of any missed words for the selection, the monitor points to the time and tells the time to the student.

The monitor then asks, "How many points do you plot for today's story?"

The monitor presents the graph to the student and directs the student by saying:

"Circle the number of the story you're recording."

    a. The monitor makes the three dots for the student before the student draws the line.

    b. The monitor directs the student to touch the dot the line is going to.

    c. The monitor directs the student to draw the line to that dot. If the student earned 1 or 2 points, the monitor praises the student for reading well.

SRA **Differentiated Reinforcement Fluency**

Decoding B1

PART 3: Materials

- **Forms and Graphs**

- **Stories**
  Baseline Stories BL-A to BL-F
  Post-Baseline Stories 1 to 45

DRF Data and Criteria Summary

Baseline to Session 15

(1) Baseline Record

Selections	Errors	Times	Pts
BL-A			1
BL-B			1
BL-C			1
BL-D			1
BL-E			1
BL-F			1
Total # of errors →	6		
Average # of errors			

← Timings

Detailed procedures for recording and summarizing data appear on pages 16–21.

NAME _____

(2) Criteria for Sessions 1–15
Based on BL-A through BL-F

Ranking by Time	Times	Pts
1		2
(2)	⬭	2
3		1
[4]	▭	1
5		0
6		0

Criteria for Sessions 1–15

Slowest time for 2 pts: ⬭

Slowest time for 1 pt: ▭

(3) Sessions 1-15 Record

Selections	Errors	Times	Pts
1			
2			
3			
4			
5			
6			
7			
8			
9			
10			
11			
12			
13			
14			
15			

Rank these six.

DRF Data and Criteria Summary

Sessions 16 to 45

(4) **Criteria for Sessions 16–30
Based on 10 through 15**

Ranking by Time	Times	Pts
1		2
②	⬭	2
3		1
4	⬜	1
5		0
6		0

Criteria for Sessions 16–30

Slowest time for 2 pts: ⬭

Slowest time for 1 pt: ⬜

(5) **Sessions 16–30 Record**

Selections	Errors	Times	Pts
16			
17			
18			
19			
20			
21			
22			
23			
24			
25			
26			
27			
28			
29			
30			

Rank these six. (spanning rows 25–30)

(6) **Criteria for Sessions 31–45
Based on 25 through 30**

Ranking by Time	Times	Pts
1		2
②	⬭	2
3		1
4	⬜	1
5		0
6		0

Criteria for Sessions 31–45

Slowest time for 2 pts: ⬭

Slowest time for 1 pt: ⬜

(7) **Sessions 31–45 Record**

Selections	Errors	Times	Pts
31			
32			
33			
34			
35			
36			
37			
38			
39			
40			
41			
42			
43			
44			
45			

Supplemental DRF Data and Criteria Summary

Criteria for Next 15 Timings
(Based on last 6 timings _____)

Ranking by Time	Times	Pts
1		2
②	(oval)	2
3		1
4	(box)	1
5		0
6		0

Criteria for next 15 sessions

Slowest time for 2 pts: (oval)

Slowest time for 1 pt: (box)

15 Sessions Record
(Use above criteria.)

Selections	Errors	Times	Pts

Criteria for Next 15 Timings
(Based on last 6 timings _____)

Ranking by Time	Times	Pts
1		2
②	(oval)	2
3		1
4	(box)	1
5		0
6		0

Criteria for next 15 sessions

Slowest time for 2 pts: (oval)

Slowest time for 1 pt: (box)

15 Sessions Record
(Use above criteria.)

Selections	Errors	Times	Pts

Practice Graph

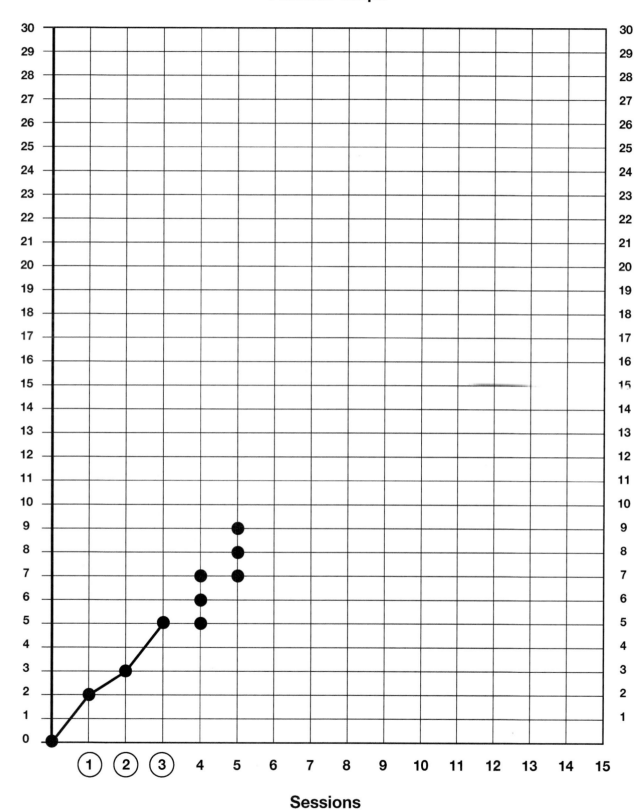

Total Points

Sessions

NAME _____

Graph for Fluency Points
Sessions 1–15

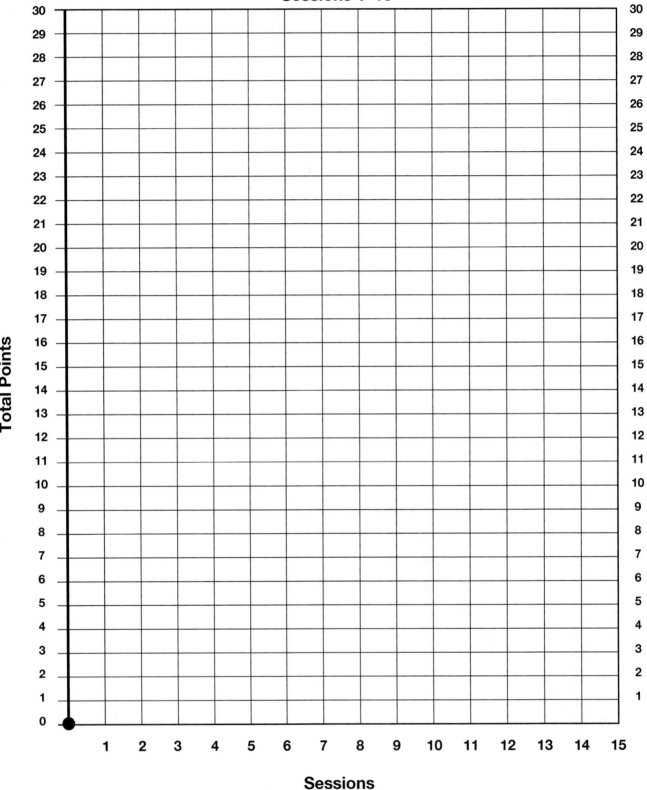

Total Points

Sessions

NAME _____

Graph for Fluency Points
Sessions 16–30

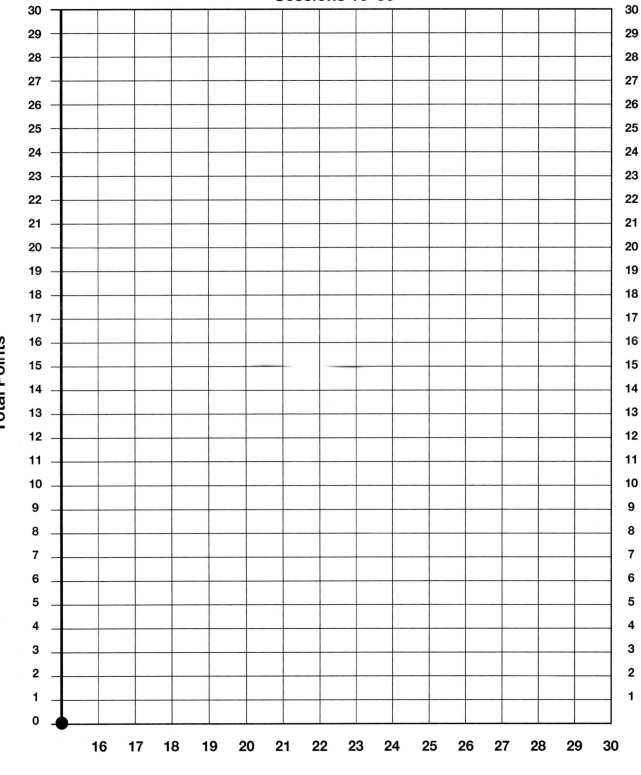

Total Points

Sessions

NAME _____

Graph for Fluency Points
Sessions 31–45

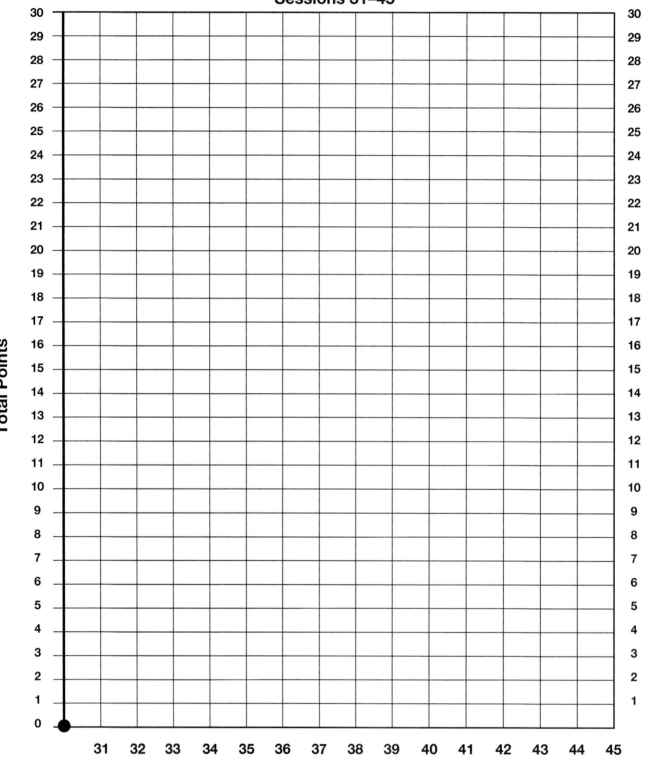

Sessions

NAME ______________________

Supplemental Graph for Fluency Points

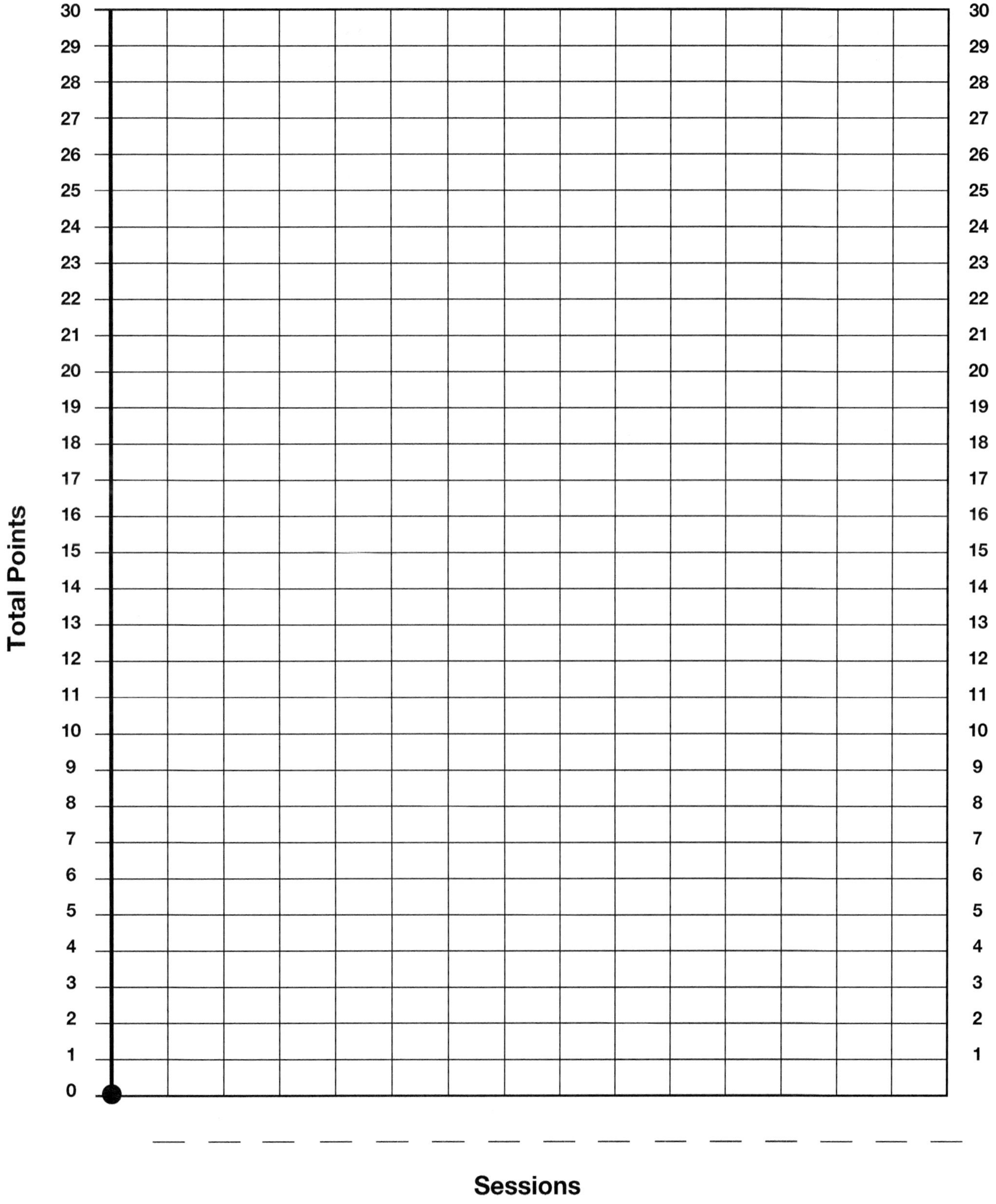

Sandy had a rat that ate fast. She said, "That rat eats too	13
much. I must make the rat slow down."	21
Sandy went to the store and got ten packs of gum. She said,	34
"I will smear the gum on the oats." Then she gave the oats to	48
the rat. "Here are some oats," she said. "You will have fun	60
eating them."	62
The rat began eating at a very fast rate. But then the rate	75
began to go down.	79
The rat chomped and chomped. The rat said, "I like oats,	90
but these oats are not fun. I am chomping as fast as I can, but	105
the oats don't go down."	110
Sandy said, "Ho, ho. There is gum on them so that you can	123
not eat at a fast rate."	129
The rat said, "Give me the oats that do not have gum on	142
them, and I will eat slowly."	148
Sandy said, "I am happy to hear that."	156
She gave the rat oats that did not have gum on them. The rat	170
did 2 things. She bit Sandy's hand. Then she ate the oats at a	184
very fast rate.	187
Sandy said, "You little rat. You told me a lie."	197
The rat said, "Yes, but did you see how fast I did it?"	210
Then Sandy said, "And you bit my hand, you little	220
rat. But I will still get you to eat slowly. You will see."	233
Sandy needed a plan, but she did not have one. So	244
she began to think of one. ★	250

Story above follows Lesson 25

Sandy's rat ate at a fast rate. The rat ran at a fast rate. And it　　16
even hopped at a fast rate. Sandy had a plan to make the rat's　　30
rate go down.　　33

Sandy got a rat that did not eat at a fast rate and did not run　　49
fast. This rat was fat. It sat and sat. When this rat ate, it　　63
chomped slowly. Sandy said, "I will take this slow rat and show　　75
my fast rat how to be slow." Sandy dropped the fat rat into the　　89
box with the fast rat.　　94

The fast rat said, "This fat rat needs help. It is too fat. I will　　109
show it how to go fast."　　115

Sandy's rat bit the fat rat on the nose. "Stop that," he said.　　128

Sandy's rat said, "Make me stop."　　134

The fat rat began to run after Sandy's rat. These rats ran and　　147
ran and ran. Then the fat rat said, "I must rest. I need to eat　　162
some oats."　　164

Sandy's rat said, "If you don't eat fast, I will eat these oats　　177
and then no oats will be left for you."　　186

"No," the fat rat said. "I can eat as fast as the next rat." And　　201
it did.　　203

The fat rat was in the box with the fast rat for seven days. At　　218
the end of the seven days, the fat rat was not fat. It was fast.　　233
When Sandy dropped oats into the box, the rats ate the oats in　　246
a flash. Then they ★ ran.　　251

Story above follows Lesson 26

A man named Champ went down a road. He came to a   12

camp. He stopped and said, "I hate to work, but I need to eat.   26

So I will see if I can get a job at this camp." So Champ went to   43

the woman who ran the camp. Champ said, "Can I work at this   56

camp? I can do lots of jobs here."   64

The camp woman said, "Are you a tramp?"   72

Champ said, "No, I am a champ at camp work."   82

"Can you fix lamps?"   86

"Yes," Champ said.   89

"Can you make boat ramps?"   94

"Yes," said Champ. "I am the champ at ramps."   103

The camp woman said, "Then I will let you work at this   115

camp." The camp woman gave Champ a hammer. She said,   125

"Take this hammer and make a ramp for these boats."   135

Champ got boards and began to hammer. When the sun went   146

down, he had made the boat ramp. He said, "Now I have to eat."   160

But the woman from the camp did not let Champ rest. She   172

handed Champ a broken lamp. Then she said, "Take these   182

clamps and fix this lamp."   187

So Champ got a clamp to hold the lamp. He fixed the lamp.   200

The camp woman said, "Now you must take a bath. I can   212

tell from your smell that you are not a champ at baths."   224

Champ said, "No, baths are not for me."   232

"You will take a bath or you will not eat," the camp woman   245

told Champ.   247

Champ ran to * the eating table.   253

Champ slept at the table. The next day he woke up and felt 13
rested. He went to the woman who ran the camp. The woman 25
held her nose as she said, "You smell, Champ. Will you take a 38
bath?" 39

"No," Champ said. 42

Just then, a big man named Sam came up. He held his nose 55
and said, "Champ, you are not the champ worker at this camp. 67
I am." 69

A woman said, "Let's have a meet between Champ and 79
Sam." 80

So the men and women set things up for the big meet. They 93
gave a tamping pole to each man. They said, "We will see how 106
well Champ can tamp." 110

They went to the hill. The camp woman said, "Take these 121
tamping poles and see how fast you can pound the ruts from 133
this path." 135

Sam and Champ began tamping. They tamped the path for 145
three miles. Sam was a very fast tamper. But Champ tamped 156
faster. The men and women did not cheer for Champ. They 167
said, "Champ can tamp fast, but Sam can make ramps faster 178
than Champ can." 181

So Champ and Sam went to the lake. The camp woman said, 193
"Each man will clamp seventy boards and hammer the boards 203
on a frame. The man with the faster rate will win this meet." 216

Sam grabbed a clamp and began clamping boards. But 225
Champ clamped faster than Sam. And Champ hammered 233
faster than Sam. 236

Sam said, "I cannot work as fast as Champ because I have to 249
keep ★ holding my nose. 253

One day a man came to the camp. This man was big and fat. 14

He smelled as bad as a goat. He went up to the camp woman 28

and said, "My name is Bob. I do not like to work, but I have to 44

eat. And I am the best worker you have seen." 54

Champ, who was champ of the camp, went up to the camp 66

woman and said, "That is Big Bob, my brother." 75

Big Bob said, "No. You can't be my brother. My brother is 87

fat, and he smells. But you are not fat, and you do not smell." 101

Champ said, "But I am your brother." 108

The camp woman said, "We do not need more workers in 119

this camp." 121

Champ said, "But you need boaters. And Big Bob is the best 133

there is." 135

The camp woman held her nose. She said, "We will see how 147

well Big Bob can do in a boat meet with Sam." 158

Each man got in a boat. But Big Bob had an old boat that 172

was very slow. 175

The camp woman said, "When I clap, begin paddling. 184

Paddle as fast as you can to the other shore of the lake." 197

The camp woman clapped, and the men began to paddle. 207

Soon Big Bob's boat was next to Sam's boat. Just then, Bob's 219

paddle broke, and Bob's boat began to slow down. Sam's boat 230

kept on going. The camp woman was standing on the lake shore. 242

She said, "Big Bob cannot beat Sam now." ★ 250

Story above follows Lesson 29

Champ and his brother Big Bob went to the shed. Champ 11
grabbed the handle of the door. He said, "This door has a lock 24
on it. How will we get in this shed? The hammers and the 37
tamping poles are in here. We need hammers and tampers if we 49
are to work." 52

Big Bob said, "Brother, don't bother with that lock. I will 63
kick the door in." 67

"No," Champ said. "Let's go to the camp woman and see if 79
she can get in this shed." 85

So they went to the camp woman. She said, "I will get a man 99
to fix that lock." 103

Later, an old man came to the camp. He had a big bag and a 118
big horn that he held to his ear. 126

He said, "I am here to fix a clock." 135

The men said, "We do not need someone to fix a clock. We 148
need someone to fix a lock. We cannot get in the shed because 161
the door is locked." 165

The old man said, "You say the door is clocked?" 175

Big Bob said, "Make a note for the old man. Even with his 188
ear horn, he cannot hear." 193

So Champ got a pen and made a note. The note said, "We 206
need to get in that shed, but the shed is locked." 217

The old man said, "I cannot help you. I work on clocks, not 230
locks." 231

So Big Bob got a pick and began to pick the lock. The lock 245
began to go, "Tick, tick, ★ tock, tock." 252

Story above follows Lesson 30

Decoding B1 49

A con man came to the camp. That con man came up the   13
camp road with a box. The camp woman met him.   23

The con man dropped his box and held the lid up. He   35
grabbed a mop from the box. He said, "The workers will like   47
this mop. It is fatter than other mops. So a worker can mop   60
faster with this mop."   64

The camp woman said, "I will get someone to take that mop   76
and see how well it works." So the camp woman yelled for   88
Champ.   89

Champ was on a slope near a shore of the lake. Was he   102
making a ramp? No, he was raking slop near the pond. He was   115
a fast slop raker. He went to the con man and the camp   128
woman. The camp woman handed the mop to Champ.   137

"Here," she said. "See if this fatter mop mops faster than   148
other mops."   150

Champ said, "I hate to stop slopping to do some mopping."   161

The camp woman said, "When I say that you must mop, you   173
must mop. So take this fat mop and begin mopping."   183

But Champ did not begin mopping. He went to the eating   194
table and said, "I will prop this mop near the door, and I will   208
sit. Then I will go back and tell the others that I mopped." So   222
that is what Champ did.   227

After he sat, he went back to the camp woman and the con   240
man. He said, "Yes, this fat mop is the best." ★   250

Story above follows Lesson 31

Cathy worked in a dress shop. One day she said, "I need a | 13
rest." So she went to her pal, Pam. She said, "Pam, let us go to | 28
hear a band play. A band is near the bend in the road. They | 42
play well." | 44

Then Cathy and Pam went to hear the band. When they got | 56
near the bend in the road, Pam said, "I need to eat. Let me | 70
lead you to a little shed. It is near the stream. They sell fish and | 85
chips in that shed." | 89

So Pam led Cathy to the fish shed near the stream. The | 101
shack was packed with folks. The folks were yelling, "I was | 112
next. Give me my order of fish and chips." | 121

Pam said, "This is a mess." | 127

Cathy and Pam left the fish shed and sat on a bench. A man | 141
came up to them. He had a net, and he was dressed in a big | 156
coat. He set the net in the sand, and then he sat down on the | 171
bench. He asked Cathy, "What is the matter?" | 179

Cathy said, "The shed is packed. We will be late to hear the | 192
band." | 193

The man said, "I am a fish packer. If you need fish, let me | 207
help you." | 209

The man went to his boat in the stream. Then he came back | 222
with a basket. Cathy said, "Let me pay you for those fish." | 234

"Give me five dollars," the man said. | 241

"That is a good deal," Cathy said. "Thank you." ★ | 250

Story above follows Lesson 32

Gretta got a little dog. She named the dog Chee. Chee got   12

bigger and bigger each day.   17

    On a very cold day, Gretta said, "Chee, I must go to the   30

store. You stay home. I will be back."   38

    Chee said, "Store, lots, of, for, no."   45

    Then Gretta said, "Did I hear that dog say things?"   55

    Chee said, "Say things can I do."   62

    Gretta said, "Dogs don't say things. So I must not hear   73

well."   74

    But Chee did say things. Gretta left the dog at home. When   86

Gretta came back, Chee was sitting near the door.   95

    Gretta said, "That dog is bigger than she was."   104

    Then the dog said, "Read, read for me of left."   114

    Gretta said, "Is that dog saying that she can read?" Gretta   125

got a pad and made a note for the dog. The note said, "Dear   139

Chee, if you can read this note, I will hand you a bag of bones."   154

    Gretta said, "Let's see if you can read."   162

    Chee said, "Dear Chee, if you can read this note, I will ham   175

you a bag for beans."   180

    Gretta said, "She can read, but she can't read well. Ho, ho."   192

    Chee became very mad. She said, "For note don't read ho ho."   204

    Gretta said, "Chee gets mad when I say ho, ho."   214

    Chee said, "Yes, no go ho ho."   221

    Then Gretta felt sad. She said, "I didn't mean to make you   233

mad. I don't like you to be sad, Chee. So I will help you say   248

things well." ★   250

Story above follows Lesson 33

The old clock maker did not hear well. He left the camp with | 13
the lock. He had this lock in his pack. He went down a road | 27
from the camp. Then he met a corn grower. | 36

But the corn grower was not a corn grower. He was the con | 49
man dressed up like a corn grower. That con man liked | 60
conning folks. | 62

The con man said, "Let's go sit in the shade near my shed." | 75

"Yes," the clock maker said, "I will trade for a bed." | 86

"No, not a bed," the con man said. "Shed. We will sit near | 99
my shed." | 101

The clock maker said, "Yes, I like a sled, but I don't see a | 115
sled." | 116

The con man was mad at the clock maker. He yelled, "WE | 128
WILL SIT IN THE SHADE." | 133

"Yes," the clock maker said. "I am ready to trade." | 143

The con man led the clock maker to the shade. He held the | 156
clock maker's horn to the clock maker's ear. Then he asked, | 167
"Will you trade your pack for some corn?" | 175

"No," the clock maker said, "I need this horn. So I will not | 188
trade this horn. But I will trade my pack for corn." | 199

The con man got a sack of corn. He set the sack near the | 213
shed. | 214

Then the con man went into that shed and got a very big | 227
horn. He said, "Hold this horn to your ear, and you will hear | 240
me better." | 242

The clock maker said, "Yes, that deal seems ★ better." | 251

Story above follows Lesson 34

Chee felt sad. So she left her home to get a job. 12

Chee went to a fire station. She went up to the man who ran 26
the station and said, "I need a job. Can you help me?" 38

The man said, "Is my hearing going bad, or did that dog say 51
something to me?" 54

The dog said, "I did say something. Do you have a job for 67
me?" 68

The man said, "Ho, ho. That dog is saying things, but dogs 80
can't speak." 82

Chee got so mad that she began to say odd things. "Fire 94
station for of to go," she said. 101

The man said, "Ho, ho. This dog is fun. I will keep this dog 115
with me. I like to hear the odd things that dog can say." 128

Chee was so mad at the fireman she said, "From of for, 140
fireman." 141

The fireman fell down and went, "Ho, ho, ho." He had tears 153
on his cheeks. His ears got red. Then he patted Chee and said, 166
"I didn't mean to make you mad. But you do say odd things." 179

Then the dog said to herself, "I will not work here. I can't 192
stand to hear that fireman go 'Ho, ho.'" 200

So Chee left the station. She went down the road to a brick 213
plant. The man in the brick plant said, "Well, well, I see a dog 227
in this plant." 230

"Yes," Chee said. Then she asked the man, "Can I have a job 243
here?" 244

The man said, "What have we ★ here?" 251

Story above follows Lesson 35

There was a big ranch in the West. The rancher who ran this   13
ranch was named Emma Branch. She rode a horse well. She   24
chopped fast, and she swam faster. The men and women who   35
worked for Emma Branch liked her. They said, "She is the best   47
in the West." On her ranch she had sheep, and she had cows.   60
There were goats and horses. There was a lot of grass.   71

The rancher had a lot of women and men working for her.   83
They worked with the sheep and the goats, and they milked the   95
cows. Each worker had a horse. But the rancher's horse was the   107
biggest and the best. It was a big, black horse named Flop.   119

Flop got its name because it reared up. When Flop reared   130
up, any rider on it fell down and went "flop" in the grass. But   144
Flop did not rear up when the rancher rode it. Emma Branch   156
bent near Flop's ear and said, "Let's go, Flop." And they went.   168
She did not have to slap the horse. She didn't have to jab her   182
heels and yell at Flop. She just said, "Let's go," and they went   195
like a shot.   198

Every day, she checked up on the workers to see what they   210
were doing. She checked to see that they were working well and   222
that they were not loafing.   227

If a worker was loafing, Emma told the worker, "I will say   239
this for the last time: 'Do not loaf on this ranch.'" ★   250

Story above follows Lesson 36

Chee went to get a job, but no plant had jobs for dogs that   14
say things. At last, Chee went to a slate plant. Chee said, "I   27
hope that I can get a job here." Chee went into the plant. Chee   41
went past stacks of slate. She came to the woman who ran the   54
plant. Chee asked, "Do you have a job I can do in this plant?"   68

The woman looked at Chee. Then the woman said, "Ho, ho,   79
ho. I cannot help going 'Ho, ho, ho.' "   87

Chee got so mad that she began to say odd things. "Stop   99
slate for from me, of go so no to do, ho ho."   111

The woman fell down and kept going "Ho, ho, ho."   121

Chee felt so mad that she did not stop saying odd things.   133

The woman got sore from going "Ho, ho." She had lots of   145
tears on her cheeks. Then she stopped ho-hoing and said, "I   156
have seen lots of things, but I have never seen a dog that said   170
odd things."   172

Chee was not so mad now. So Chee began to say things that   185
made sense. Chee said, "I told you not to go 'Ho, ho.' I told you   200
that I need a job."   205

The woman got up and clapped her hands. She said, "Let me   217
see. I think I may have a job for you." The woman's cheeks still   231
had tears on them. She asked, "Can you stack slate?"   241

Chee said, "I think so."   246

She showed Chee how. ★   250

Story above follows Lesson 37

Emma Branch had a lot of big sheep on her ranch. One day   13
she said, "My sheep need shearing. I will send for a sheep   25
shearer."   26

So she told one of her helpers to go to town and get someone   40
who can shear sheep. The helper went down the road to town.   52
But he did not get there. He met the con man on the road. The   67
con man said, "Where are you going?"   74

The helper said, "The rancher needs her sheep sheared."   83

The con man said, "I am the best at shearing sheep. I have   96
shears in my pack."   100

So Emma's helper led the con man back to the ranch. When   112
they got there, Emma yelled from the door, "I hope that man   124
can shear fast."   127

The con man said, "I can shave sheep. I can shape. And I   140
can shear."   142

"But how is your rate at shearing?" the rancher asked.   152

"I can go so fast that I can shave a sheep before it sees the   167
shears. You can shop and shop, but you cannot get someone   178
who can shape or shave faster than me."   186

So the con man got the job. He told the rancher to get him   200
ten sacks for holding the wool.   206

The con man had a plan. He did not plan to shear sheep. He   220
planned to steal sheep. He planned to pack sheep into sacks.   231
Then he planned to take those sacks and run from the ranch.   243

But his plan did not work very ★ well.   251

Champ had worked at the camp for nearly a year. He had   12
tamped and made ramps. He had fixed lamps and raked slop   23
near the lake. But now he said, "I think I will leave this camp.   38
I am a champ, and champs don't stay in the same camp for more   51
than a year."   54

So Champ got his pack and went to the camp woman. He   66
told her, "I must go now. The work here is getting old, and I   80
need a rest. I will go sit in the shade and eat beans and rest. It   96
is time to go where I do not have to take a bath."   109

So Champ left and went down the camp road. When he got   121
to a town, he said, "I see a person on a big black horse. I will   137
ask that rider where I can go to rest in the shade." Champ went   151
up to the person on the black horse and said, "Tell me, where   164
can I go to rest in the shade?"   172

The person on the horse was Emma Branch. She was the   183
rancher that shaved the con man. She said, "I help men and   195
women who work well."   199

"I work well," Champ said. "But I am sick of working. I need   212
a rest."   214

Then the rancher said to Champ, "I can tell that you do not   227
like to work. Are you a tramp?"   234

That made Champ mad. He said, "I am a champ, not a tramp.   247
I like to ★ work."   251

The sun came up in the morning. Champ was sleeping near a 12
big sheep shed. The rancher's helper came to wake him up. 23

Champ said, "Leave me be. I am sleeping." So Champ went 34
back to sleep. 37

The helper ran to Emma and said, "That Champ didn't get 48
up when I went to wake him up." 56

Emma grabbed shears and ran over to Champ. Her helper 66
ran with her. When they got to Champ, the rancher handed her 78
shears to her helper. She said to Champ, "If you don't get up, 91
my helper will give you a shearing." 98

So Champ got up and went to the sheep shed with Emma. 110

Emma said, "We have a deal. If you can shear 50 sheep as 123
fast as you hammer, you may stay and rest on my ranch." 135

Then she handed the shears to Champ. Champ felt more like 146
sleeping than shearing. He said, "I did not sleep well. When I 158
am not rested, I cannot work well. I will have to jump up and 172
down to wake up." So Champ began to jump up and down. 184
Then he said, "Now I can shear sheep." 192

"Good," Emma said. "You have 50 minutes to shear 50 202
sheep." Like a flash, Champ went for a sheep. 211

He grabbed the sheep and sat on its nose. His shears flashed 223
in the sun. And wool went plop, plop from the sheep. The 235
rancher said, "Wow! That's fast shearing. This man has made 245
heaps and heaps of wool." ★ 250

Story above follows Lesson 40

Champ had stayed at the ranch for seven weeks. Every day, he 12
had big meals of beef and ham and beans and corn. Every day, 25
he sat in the shade near the lake. And every day, he got a little 40
slower. He got slower and slower with each meal that he ate. 52

The rancher did not think that Champ was slow. She had 63
seen him go so fast that the helper did not sweep the wool as 77
fast as Champ shaved sheep. 82

Emma went to town and bragged. She said, "There is a man on 95
my ranch who can shear sheep faster than anyone you have seen." 107

When Emma was in town one day, she told a lot of people, 120
"A man on my ranch can beat anyone in a shearing meet." 132

A woman named Shelly stepped up to Emma and said, "I 143
think I can beat anyone in a shearing meet." 152

"Let's have a meet," the others yelled. 159

"Yes," the rancher said. 163

So they set up a meet between Champ and Shelly. A man 175
said, "Let's make bets. I will bet on Shelly. I have seen her 188
work with shears, and I think she can beat any other worker." 200

The rancher said, "I will bet ten dollars on my champ." Then 212
she made other bets. 216

When Emma got back to the ranch, she told Champ, "Your 227
seven weeks are up. If you stay, you will have to work." 239

"That is a shame," he said. "So I will have to ★ leave." 251

Story above follows Lesson 41

The rancher had told Champ to get in shape for the shearing   12

meet. But did Champ get in shape? No. He ate big meals of   25

corn and ham and beans and meat. Then he went to sleep.   37

Was Champ in shape at the end of the week? No. Champ   49

was out of shape and very slow.   56

People from town came to the ranch with Shelly. Shelly was   67

in tip-top shape. Before the meet began, she sheared a sheep to   79

show the others how fast she was. Before the wool that fell from   92

the sheep had landed, that sheep was shaved from one end to   104

the other.   106

The people cheered. "Shelly can beat anyone at shearing,"   115

they yelled.   117

Champ had to work to pick up the shears. He said, "I may   130

have rested too much, but when I get going, I will speed up."   143

The rancher said, "Shelly and Champ will shear all day."   153

Champ said to his helper, "I hope you are fast at sweeping.   165

This wool will be dropping very fast."   172

The rancher said, "Go," and the shearing began.   180

Champ's shears did not go like a flash. And the wool did not   193

pile up fast. "I must go faster," he said. But he did not go faster.   208

He went slower. He ran the shears into the sheep's ear, and the   221

sheep bit him on the leg. Then the sheep got up and ran from   235

the shed.   237

The people said, "Ho, ho. Champ can't shear. But Shelly is   248

going like ★ a shot."   252

Champ worked and worked at the ranch. Every day, he got   11
up when the sun was peeking over the hill in the east. Champ   24
did not eat a big meal. He went to the sheep shed and sheared   38
sheep. Then he picked corn. Then he ate a little meal. He had   51
an egg and a little bit of ham. He said, "I need more to eat."   66

"No more," the rancher said. "Back to work for you." She   77
handed Champ a hammer. "Take boards and make a gate," she   88
said.   89

After Champ had made a gate, the rancher said, "Now take   100
boards and make a pen for goats." After Champ had made a   112
pen of boards, she said, "Next, you're going to dig holes for   124
planting trees."   126

So Champ dug ten tree holes. Then he planted three trees.   137
Then he sheared more sheep. At last, the rancher said, "Now   148
you may eat a meal."   153

But it was a very little meal. Champ ate it and said, "I need   167
more to eat."   170

"No more," she said. And she gave Champ more work.   180

At the end of the day, Champ was sore. He was sore the next   194
day.   195

But at the end of the week, he began to get faster. His hammer   209
began to go like a flash. His shears began to get hot when he was   224
shaving sheep. Champ was beginning to get back in shape.   234

Champ worked for five weeks. And he got a little faster every   246
week that he worked. ★   250

Story above follows Lesson 43

Champ felt he was in shape for the shearing meet. When   11
there was no more work on Emma's ranch, Champ did some   22
work at the next ranch, so he could stay in shape. He made ten   36
gates. He planted 600 trees. He sheared 950 sheep. The helpers   47
that worked on this ranch said, "He is the fastest worker in the   60
land."   61

Shelly did not get in shape. She said, "I am in shape. My   74
hands are fast. I have never been beaten in a shearing meet."   86

On the day of the meet, Champ sat near the ranch gate. The   99
people from town came up the road. They waved to Champ.   110

The people said, "We made bets that Shelly will beat you."   121
Then they went to the sheep shed and waited.   130

When Shelly came up the road, the people cheered. "Here's   140
Shelly," they yelled.   143

Just before the meet began, Emma Branch came up to   153
Champ. She said, "If you do not beat Shelly, I will not let you   167
stay here. You will have to get your things and leave this ranch."   180

Champ didn't say a thing. He just sat and waited.   190

"We are ready for a shearing meet," a woman yelled. "Let's go."   202

Champ ran fast as a shot. He grabbed his shears and said, "I   215
will need three helpers. I will make heaps of wool so fast that 2   229
helpers will not keep up with me."   236

The others said, "Ho, ho." Seven people said, "We will help   247
you with wool." ★   250

Story above follows Lesson 44

Chee worked as a slate stacker for nearly a year. By then, her | 13
rate of stacking was very good. But she was getting a little sick | 26
of her job. "Stack, stack, stack," she said. "It's time to do | 38
something else." So she went to the woman who ran the slate | 50
plant and said, "I think I have to quit and get another job." | 63

The woman said, "You have been a good worker. Good luck." | 74

Chee left the plant and went looking for work. She came to a | 87
sleeve plant. They made sleeves for coats in this plant. | 97

Chee went into the plant and said to the people working in a | 110
big room, "Where is the person who runs this plant?" | 120

They went, "Ho, ho. We do not work for a person." | 131

Chee told them, "You must work for someone. Show me who." | 142

A man stepped up to Chee. The man said, "Step into that | 154
room and you will see who runs this plant. His name is Rop." | 167

So Chee stepped into the room. Then she stopped. There was | 178
no man seated at the desk. There was a yellow dog at the desk. | 192

The yellow dog slapped a stamp on a letter. Then he pressed | 204
a button. A man came into the room. The yellow dog said, "I | 217
have stamped this letter. Get it into the mail box now." | 228

The man grabbed the letter and ran from the room. "Don't | 239
slam the door," the yellow dog yelled. | 246

The man did not ★ slam the door. | 253

Story above follows Lesson 45

Chee had met a yellow dog in a sleeve plant. The yellow dog | 13
was named Rop, and he ran the plant. He said that he was | 26
better than Chee at doing things. Chee got mad. So a meet was | 39
set between Rop and Chee. Rop said, "We will see if you can | 52
beat me in this meet." | 57

Rop yelled to the workers in the sleeve plant. "Stop sleeving | 68
and get in here fast," he said. The workers ran into the room. | 81
Rop said, "Chee and I are going to have a meet. We will begin | 95
by seeing how fast we can eat." | 102

Rop told a worker, "Get me 2 slabs of fresh meat. Drop the | 115
slabs on the scale and see that they are the same." | 126

A woman ran from the plant. She went to the store. She | 138
grabbed 2 slabs of meat that were on sale. She got back to the | 152
plant and dropped them on the scale. Each slab was the same. | 164

Rop handed a slab to Chee. "Here's your slab. See if you can | 177
keep up with me." Then he said, "When you hear me say, 'Go,' | 190
get your teeth into that meat. Get set . . ." | 198

Chee was ready to eat. She was not going to let that yellow | 211
dog beat her at eating meat. | 217

"Go," Rop said. And Chee went. Chomp, chomp, gromp, clop. | 227

But Chee did not beat Rop, and Rop did not beat Chee. | 239
Their score was the same and that made Rop very mad. ★ | 250

Chee and Rop went into the sleeve-making room of the   10
plant. There Rop said, "I will get the best score for this meet.   23
We will see how fast that lap dog can slap sleeves on coats. The   37
dog that slaps sleeves fastest will get the best score."   47

Rop handed Chee a needle. Rop said, "Take this needle and   58
get set to go. And don't stab yourself. Ho, ho."   68

Chee was mad. She held the needle and waited for Rop to   80
say, "Go."   82

Rop said, "Get set . . . go."   87

Chee went very fast, but she stabbed herself with the needle.   98
"Ow," she said.   101

"Ho, ho," Rop said, "That lap dog just stabbed herself. Ho,   112
ho, ho, hee, hee." As Rop was ho-heeing, he did not see where   125
his needle was going, and he stabbed himself. "Ow," he said.   136

"Ho, hee, hep, hep, hep," Chee said.   143

Rop yelled, "Stop. This meet is over. I have slapped seven   154
sleeves on coats. So I am the champ, and I get the best score.   168
Let's hear it for me."   173

"Stop," Chee said. "I have slapped seven sleeves on coats,   183
too. So my score is the same as yours."   192

Chee was sore where the needle went into her, but she was   204
glad that Rop had stabbed himself, too. Rop said, "Let's go to   216
the room where we form sleeves."   222

Chee, Rop, and the others went to the sleeve-forming room.   232
Rop handed Chee shears. Then he handed her a form for   243
making sleeves. He said, "Slap this form ★ on the wool."   253

Story above follows Lesson 47

Kit made a boat. She made the boat of tin. The nose of the   14
boat was very thin. Kit said, "I think that this boat is ready for   28
me to take on the lake." So Kit went to the lake with her boat.   43

Her boat was a lot of fun. It went fast. But when she went to   58
dock it at the boat ramp, she did not slow it down. And the   72
thin nose of the boat cut a hole in the boat ramp.   84

The man who sold gas at the boat ramp got mad. He said,   97
"That boat cuts like a blade. Do not take the boat on this lake   111
any more. Take it where you will not run into things."   122

So Kit did not take her boat to the lake any more. She went   136
to the sea with her boat. She said, "There is a lot of room in the   152
sea. I will not run this boat into any docks."   162

So Kit went on the sea with her boat. The nose of her boat   176
went into the waves like a blade. Kit's boat went faster and   188
faster. She said, "I am a good sailor."   196

After a while, she did not see the shore of the sea any more.   210
So Kit went to the left. She said, "I think this is the way back   225
to shore." But now the boat was on its way to Japan.   237

A fog came in. It was thick. Kit did not see a thing. ★   250

Story above follows Lesson 48

Kit's boat was in the middle of the sea. It had made a hole in   15
a big ship. The big ship went down. Seventeen men, 47 women,   27
three dogs, and a pet goat got in Kit's boat. So Kit made holes   41
in the bottom of the boat to drain the water from the boat.   54

And the water did begin to drain, but not very fast. Kit said,   67
"These holes are not letting water out faster than water is   78
coming in the boat. We need a bigger hole in the bottom."   90

A sailor said, "We left our tools on board the big ship, so we   104
have no way to make bigger holes."   111

A man said, "So let's just yell for help. HELP, HELP."   122

"Hush up," Kit said. "We will get back to shore if we just   135
keep our heads and think of a way to make a big hole that will   150
drain water very fast."   154

An old woman said, "My pet goat likes to eat tin. Maybe he   167
can eat a hole in the bottom of this tin boat."   178

"Yes," Kit said. "Let's see what that goat can do." Then she   190
ordered everybody to make room for the goat to eat. "Eat," Kit   202
said.   203

And the goat did begin to eat, but it didn't eat the tin boat. It   218
ate a man's wool sleeve. "Stop that," he yelled. "Eat tin, not wool."   231

Kit said, "Yes, don't let that goat get filled up on wool. It   244
won't have any room for tin." ★   250

This is another story about Kit and her tin boat. Kit had her   13
boat at the dock. She was fixing the hole that the goat made in   27
the boat. She painted her boat green. Then she asked the man   39
who sold gas at the dock, "Where can I get some big rocks?"   52

The man said, "Why do you need big rocks?"   61

Kit said, "I will drop them in the front of my boat."   73

The man asked, "Why will you do that?"   81

Kit said, "So that my boat will go faster. I don't like boats   94
that go slow."   97

The man said, "How will the rocks in the front of your boat   110
make the boat go faster?"   115

Kit said, "Don't you see? The rocks will make the front of   127
my boat lower than the back of my boat. So my boat will be   141
going downhill. Things go very fast when they go downhill."   151

The man said, "Ho, ho. Those rocks will just make your   162
boat go slower."   165

But Kit got rocks and dropped them in the front of her boat.   178
Then she said, "Now it is time to see how fast this boat will run."   193

The front of the boat was very low in the water. When Kit let go   208
of the rope, the boat began to go—faster and faster. It went over   222
the waves like a streak. It went faster than the big speed boats. It   236
went faster than any boat on the sea. But it began to turn left. ★   250

Story above follows Lesson 50

Decoding B1 69

Kit was in bad shape. She said, "I can fix things up."   12

The cop said, "Do not try to bribe us. This is a crime."   25

Kit said to her, "I was not trying to bribe you. But you must   39
help me. I need yellow paint."   45

The cop said, "Why do you need yellow paint?"   54

Kit said, "Get me the paint, and you will see."   64

So the cop got another cop to run for the paint. The cop   77
stepped in front of Kit and said, "Do not try to leave." When the   91
other cop came back with the can of yellow paint, Kit smiled.   103

Then she took the lid from the can and began to paint her   116
boat yellow.   118

"What are you doing?" the cops asked. "How can it help   129
anything to paint that boat yellow?"   135

Kit grinned and said, "You will see."   142

Kit got in the boat, and the boat began to float up into the   156
sky. The cops said, "Do you see what I see? That boat is   169
floating in the sky."   173

Kit smiled. Then she hollered down to the cops, "Goodbye."   183

The cops hollered, "Why is that boat floating?"   191

Kit said, "You see, the boat was green, and now it is yellow.   204
Yellow is lighter than green. Now the boat is so light that it   217
floats in the sky."   221

The boat sailed over a town. Then it turned and sailed over   233
the bay. Then it began to sail over the open sea.   244

Kit smiled and said, "Now I ★ will get my green paint."   255

Story above follows Lesson 51

Henry had a hot rod. He ran his hot rod very fast down the   14
freeway. But he ran it too fast, and—wham!—there went his   26
cam shaft. Henry said, "Now my hot rod will not go."   37

A truck came and dragged Henry's hot rod back to a motor   49
shop. The shop man looked at the motor. Then he rubbed his   61
chin. He said, "I don't think I can get to this job for three   75
weeks. When do you need this heap?"   82

Henry said, "That hot rod is not a heap. Why can't you get   95
to it now?"   98

The shop man rubbed his chin. Then he said, "I don't have   110
time."   111

The shop man said, "I have three other jobs. When I get   123
them fixed, I can work on your rod."   131

Henry said, "Where can I take my hot rod to get it fixed now?"   145

The shop man said, "There is no shop in town that can do   158
the work now. They have lots of jobs."   166

"Why is that?" Henry asked.   171

"Because people go too fast when they go down the   181
freeway," the shop man said.   186

Henry said, "I will not wait. I will fix my motor at home."   199

"That seems like the best thing to do," the shop man said. "I   212
can't do the job here, so why not do it at home?"   224

"That is what I will do," Henry said.   232

The shop man asked, "Have you ever fixed a motor?"   242

"No," Henry said. "But that will not stop ★ me."   251

Story above follows Lesson 52

Henry got a book on fixing motors. Henry went home with   11
the book. He sat in his hot rod and looked at the words in the   26
book, but Henry did not know how to read those words.   37

Here is what it said in the book: "There are three bolts that   50
hold this end of the cam shaft."   57

Here is what Henry was reading: "Where are there belts that   68
hold this end for a came shaft."   75

Henry said, "What does that mean?"   81

He kept reading. Here is what it said in his book: "When you   94
take the seals from the shaft, you press on them and then lift   107
them from the shaft."   111

This is what Henry said when he was reading those words: 122
"Why take and steal I dress and then lifted them of the shaft."   135

Henry said, "I don't know what this book means." He tossed   146
the book down and said, "I don't need a book to fix this motor.   160
I have seen people work on motors, and I don't think it will be   174
a very big job."   178

So Henry began to work on his motor. While he was taking   190
some bolts from the motor, a flat strip fell on his foot. "Ow!" he   204
yelled.   205

Then he took some other bolts from the motor, and the   216
motor fell on his foot. "Ow," he yelled. He jumped up and   228
down and yelled some more.   233

His sister, Molly, came through the doorway. "What did you   243
do?" Molly asked. "Why are you yelling?" ★   250

Story above follows Lesson 53

Henry was trying to fix his motor, but he was not doing very
well. He was looking at the words in his book on motors, but
Henry did not know what they said. The book said: "To turn a
cam shaft, you file each cam."   13 26 39 45

But this is what Henry said as he was reading: "To turn a
cam shaft, you fill each cam."   58 64

Henry said, "What does that mean?" He tossed the book
aside and said, "That book is not helping me very much. I can
do the job myself." So Henry worked and worked.   74 87 96

After a while, his motor was in little bits. Now he did not
have a motor. He had a heap of steel.   109 118

"Where is the cam shaft?" he asked as he looked at the big
pile of steel.   131 134

He picked up a big gear. "Is this a cam shaft?" he asked. He
ran his hand over the teeth of the gear. "These things must be
the cams," he said.   148 161 165

Henry was looking at the gear when a truck came down the
street. The truck was dragging his sister's hot rod.   177 186

Molly was mad. She ran over to Henry and said, "Where is
that book? My motor broke down, and I've got to fix it fast."   198 211

Molly grabbed the book. She ran to her hot rod and began
to work.   223 225

When it was time for dinner, Molly had fixed her hot rod.
She had taken the pan and taken three bent rods from the motor. ★   237 250

Kit said, "I think I will get rid of this boat. It makes ships   14
sink. It has ripped up 2 docks. It has made paths and trenches.   27
It tore holes in the bank, and that is a bad crime."   39

Kit had a lot to gripe over. So she said, "I will sell the boat."   54
She made a note and stuck it on the side of the tin boat. The   69
note said: 71

FOR SALE. A TIN BOAT   76
I WILL TRADE FOR A BIKE.   82

The con man was in town. He had five tires. Each tire had a   96
hole in it.   99

The con man said, "I will sit at this site until I see someone   113
to con." So he sat down on the tires. He was very tired.   126

While he rested, Kit came up the dock. The con man said to   139
himself, "If I can con this woman, I can get rid of my tires.   153
Then I will get some pike to eat. I like fish."   164

The con man said, "I have some fine tires if you have   176
something to trade."   179

Kit said, "I have a boat to trade, but I don't like to trade for   194
tires. I need a bike."   199

The con man said, "Trade your boat for these tires. Then   210
you can take these tires and trade them for a bike."   221

Kit said, "That seems like a good thing to do."   231

The con man said, "Get a grip on these tires, and let's hike   244
down to your boat." So Kit ★ grabbed the tires.   253

The con man had traded his clock, his cash, his ring, and | 12
five tires with holes in them for Kit's tin boat. | 22

Now the con man was ready to become the best bank robber | 34
in the West. He said, "I will pile rocks in the nose of this boat. | 49
The more rocks I pile, the faster it will go. So I will make this | 64
boat the fastest thing there is." | 70

So the con man slid the boat into deep water near the dock. | 83
Then the con man got a big pile of rocks. He dropped ten rocks | 97
into the nose of the boat. Then he dropped ten more. | 108

He said, "Now this boat will go very fast." The nose of the | 121
boat was low in the water. | 127

The con man heaped ten more rocks into the nose of the | 139
boat. Then he said, "Now this boat will . . . sink." And it did. | 151
The nose of the boat went down. And "glub, blub," the boat | 163
went to the bottom of the sea. | 170

The con man made a deal with a skin diver. The con man | 183
gave the skin diver a coat. | 189

The skin diver went under the water and lifted the pile of | 201
rocks from the boat. Then the boat began to float. | 211

The con man said, "This time, I will not heap so many rocks | 224
in the nose of this boat." So the con man dropped six rocks | 237
into the nose. He hopped into the boat and said, "I will | 249
fly ★ over the waves." | 253

The con man was zipping here and there in Kit's tin boat.   12
The boat went into a fish-packing plant, into a taffy plant, and   24
into a cotton mill. The con man was a mess. He had a mess of   39
cotton taffy pike in his boat. The steering wheel had taffy on it.   52

The con man said, "I must go somewhere and hide. I must   64
throw the rocks out of this boat so that it will slow down."   77

He began tossing cotton taffy rocks from the nose of the   88
boat. The boat went slower and slower. Then the con man   99
began heaving the pile of pike from the boat. Soon the main   111
street of the town had cotton taffy on it. The boat began to   124
slow down.   126

The con man said, "Now I will run and hide before the cops   139
come here." But when he went to slip from the boat, he said, "I   153
am sticking to the seat. This taffy will not let go of me."   166

The cops and their nine dogs ran up to the con man. The   179
man from the dock ran up to him. The man hollered, "That is   192
the man who smashed my dock into bits."   200

The woman from the fish-packing plant ran up to the con   211
man. The fish packer said, "That is the man who made a hole   224
in my plant. He zipped away with a boatload of striped pike."   236

The man from the taffy factory came running up the street.   247
He yelled, "Stop ★ that man."   252

Story above follows Lesson 57

The con man made everybody think that he was from space. 11

He was a big mass of cotton lint. The cotton lint was sticking 24

to the taffy. And the taffy was sticking to the con man's skin. It 38

was sticking to everything. The con man said to himself, "I will 50

give these people the scare of their lives." 58

He held up his hands and said a deep "Rrrrr." 68

Three dogs went, "Ooowww," and ran down the street. 77

Then the con man said, "I am from space, and I will get you." 91

The dock man said, "I'm going to run to the sea and dive 104

in." That is what he did. So did the people from the plants. 117

The cops said, "Let's not make this space thing mad." They 128

smiled at him. 131

The con man said, "Rrrrr. I will get you." He began to go for 145

the cops. 147

The cops said, "We had better leave this spot." And they did. 159

They ran down the street and—splash!—they dived into the sea. 171

The con man was standing in the middle of the street. 182

Nobody was near him. He said, "Wow! This is fun. I think I'll 195

go into the bank and see if I can pick up some bags of gold." 210

The con man said, "I will go into the bank." The con man 223

didn't see well. His nose was a mass of cotton lint. So the con 237

man didn't see a striped pike in front of the bank. 248

Slip! Plop! ★ 250

Story above follows Lesson 58

It was raining, and the con man was griping about the rain. 12

He said, "My plan is going down the drain." 21

He was trying to run with the three bags of gold, but they 34

were not light, and he did not run fast. The cotton in his hair 48

was running down his nose. He did not see where he was going. 61

He slipped on a pile of slippery pike and—plop, plop, plop!— 73

the con man hit the street, and the three bags of gold landed on 87

the con man. 90

A little boy was standing near the con man. The boy said, 102

"You are not from space. I can see that you are just a wet man." 117

The lint was sliding from the con man's hair, from his hands, 129

from his nose, and from his coat. The rain was coming down 141

very fast, and the con man was very, very wet. 151

A dog ran up to the con man and began to lick the taffy 165

from his hand. "Don't bite me," the con man said. And the dog 178

did not bite. It licked and licked. It liked the taffy. Then three 191

cats came up to the con man. They began to lick the taffy. 204

Then five dogs and nine goats came over and began licking 215

taffy. 216

"I don't like this," the con man said. He was trying to get up. 230

He said, "I must get to the other side of the street." But he 244

slipped on a striped pike and ★—plop! 251

Story above follows Lesson 59

There was a bug. That bug liked to dig. He dug and dug. His | 14
mother said, "Why do you keep digging? The rest of us bugs | 26
eat leaves and sit in the shade. But you dig and dig." | 38

"When I dig, I feel happy," the digging bug said. "I like to | 51
make holes." | 53

So he made holes. When he stopped digging, he was dusty. | 64
His brothers and sisters said, "You are a mess. You have dust | 76
on your back. What are you doing?" | 83

The bug said, "When I dig, I feel happy." And so that bug | 96
dug and dug. | 99

Then something happened. The days began to get hotter and | 109
hotter. The sun was so hot that the other bugs said, "We | 121
cannot stay here. It is too hot. We must go to a spot that is not | 137
so hot." | 139

They walked here and there, but they did not find a spot that | 152
felt cool. Then they came to a big hole in the side of a hill. They | 168
said, "Let's go down this hole. It looks cool inside." | 178

The bugs went inside the hole. Then the mother bug stopped. | 189
She said, "Did you hear that? I hear something in this hole." | 201

The other bugs stopped. Then one of them said, "Yes, I hear | 213
something. I think I hear digging." | 219

So the bugs began to sneak down the hole. Soon they came | 231
to a bend in the hole. The mother bug said, "Stay here, and I | 245
will check out the digging." ★ | 250

Story above follows Lesson 60

The dusty bug was resting in his mine. It was hot outside. He   13
had a rusty shovel. He had been digging with the shovel, but   25
now he was tired. He said, "I need to eat. I like dill pickles, but   40
I don't have any dills."   45

He tossed the shovel to one side. Then he came out of his   58
mine. The sun was very hot. The bug went to a store. Then he   72
picked up a tub of pickles. He said to the clerk, "Will you bill   86
me for these dill pickles?"   91

The clerk said, "No, we do not bill for pickles. You must pay   104
cash in this store."   108

The bug said, "I don't have cash with me. But if you send me   122
a bill, I will pay for it."   129

The clerk said, "You did not hear me. I said that we do not   143
bill for dill pickles."   147

The bug said, "That's fine with me. Now that I smell these   159
pickles, I can tell that they are rotten."   167

"They are not rotten," the clerk said. "They are the best   178
pickles in town."   181

The bug began to laugh. Then he said, "These pickles are so   193
bad that they will make you sick if you eat them."   204

The clerk ran over to the bug. The clerk said, "Give me one   217
of those pickles. I'll show you that they are good."   227

The bug handed the pickle to the clerk. The clerk chomped   238
on the pickle. Then the clerk smiled. "That dill is fine," she ★ said. 251

Story above follows Lesson 61

The old clock maker liked to work with plants when he 11
wasn't working with clocks. He had lots of plants in back of his 24
home. Every day after work, he dressed in a bib and went to 37
dabble with his plants. While he dabbled, he talked. He didn't 48
hear himself, so he didn't know that he was saying things very 60
loudly. When he came to a plant that did not have buds, he 73
said, "This plant is a dud because it doesn't have one bud." 85

One day, he was dabbling and talking when his wife came 96
out. She said, "A woman is here. Can you make a bid on fixing 110
a clock?" 112

The old clock maker did not hear her. The clock maker said, 124
"I do not have a rip in my bib." 133

His wife said, "I did not say 'bib,' I said 'bid.' A woman 146
needs a bid. Can you tell her how much she will have to pay?" 160

"I'm not going to the bay," the clock maker said. "I'm going 172
to stay here with the bees and my plants." 181

"Come with me," his wife said. "I will let you speak to the 194
woman." So she led the old clock maker inside. 203

A woman was standing near the door. She was holding a big 215
clock. The woman said, "When this clock works, a deer runs 226
out every hour, and the clock goes, 'ding, ding.' But the clock 238
does not work. The deer does not come out, and the clock ★ goes, 251
'bing, bing.' " 253

Story above follows Lesson 62

The clock maker gave a bid on the clock that he had   12

dropped. He made a bid of eleven dollars. Then he took the   24

clock to his work room. In that room he had lots of clocks.   37

Every hour, the clocks went, "dong, dong," and, "ding, ding."   47

But the clock maker did not hear them.   55

In the work room, the clock maker had a bin of parts from   68

other clocks. He also had a lot of tools for fixing clocks.   80

The clock maker held the clock with the deer. He said, "I   92

will have to paint this clock." So he got a brush and dabbed   105

paint on the clock.   109

He made the clock orange. Then he dabbed paint on the   120

deer. He made the deer yellow.   126

Then he went to his bin of old clocks to look for one that   140

had a good deer. He looked and looked. Then he began to talk   153

to himself. He said, "This is bad. I made a bid on fixing this   167

clock, but I cannot see another clock with a working deer. The   179

best I can see is a clock with a working frog. That frog comes   193

out every hour and bobs up and down."   201

The clock maker took the parts from the clock with the frog   213

and slapped them into the clock with the deer.   222

At the end of an hour, the deer came out and bobbed up and   236

down like a frog. The clock maker was happy. Five clocks in his   249

bin ★ had good dingers.   253

The clock maker had painted a clock orange. He had made   11
the deer yellow. He had fixed the deer so that it bobbed up and   25
down like a frog. When the clock maker took the clock to the   38
woman, the woman got very mad. She tossed the clock down.   49
The clock maker took the broken clock back to his shop. He   61
was going to fix it again.   67

He had just put his work bib on when his wife came in. She   81
said, "Did you just come in?"   87

"Yes," the clock maker said, "I can grin." And he did.   98

His wife shook her head. Then she said, "A little girl is   110
outside. She wants to know if she can pick weeds in your   122
garden."   123

The clock maker said, "There are no seeds in my garden.   134
The plants are just getting buds. They won't have seeds before   145
the end of summer."   149

"Not seeds," his wife said. "Weeds. The girl wants to pick   160
weeds."   161

"Why does she want to lick weeds?" the clock maker asked.   172

His wife was getting mad. She said, "I will tell her that she   185
can pick weeds. If she does a good job, I will pay her ten   199
dollars."   200

"That's fine," the clock maker said. "But you don't have to   211
holler."   212

His wife walked from the room. Then the old clock maker   223
wiped his hands on his bib. "Time to go to work," he said.   236

He grabbed the broken deer clock and began to set it on his   249
work ★ table.   251

Story above follows Lesson 64

The clock maker had taken an alligator from a dusty old   11
clock and had slapped it into the deer clock. The alligator was   23
yellow, and it had antlers. The old man said, "This clock looks   35
just like it did before."   40

So the clock maker took the clock to the woman. The clock   52
maker rapped on her door. The woman came to the door.   63
"What do you want?" she said.   69

"Here it is," the clock maker said. He held up the alligator   81
clock. "This clock is fixed up as good as ever."   91

The woman looked at the clock and said, "Oh, no. I don't want   104
to buy dusty clocks with beads on them. I had a good clock,   117
and you busted that clock. Now you are selling old junk clocks."   129

"Yes," the old clock maker said. "It looks just as good as   141
ever. Here, hold it while I set the hands."   150

Before the woman was able to back away, the clock maker   161
handed her the clock and began to set the hands. As soon as   174
the hands were set for five o'clock, the clock made a loud   186
sound. "Blip, blop," sounded the bell.   192

And here came the alligator. It bobbed up and down. It   203
bobbed this way and that way. It ran around the front of the   216
clock. Then it bit the woman's finger.   223

"Ouch!" yelled the woman. She dropped the clock. The   232
alligator grabbed her foot. The paint on the alligator was wet,   243
and now the woman's foot had a * yellow spot.   252

When we left the con man, he was in the hospital. He had   13
told the cops and the jailer that he was sick. He really wasn't   26
sick. He was just playing sick. But the cop took him to the   39
hospital. The cop went up to a nurse and said, "Nurse, I have a   53
sick man. He needs help."   58

The nurse said, "We will fix him up fast." She had the con   71
man sit on a cart. Then she took the con man to a room.   85

As soon as she left the room, the con man darted for the   98
door. He peeked outside. But the cop was standing near the   109
door. "Nuts," the con man said. "I will try the window."   120

He darted to the window. He grabbed the handles and   130
opened it wide. Then he looked out. There were bars on the   142
window. "Nuts," the con man said.   148

He sat on the bed and said to himself, "I must think of a trick   163
that will get me out of here." Suddenly he jumped up. "I've got   176
it," he yelled. Then he began to bark like a dog. He had a plan.   191

The nurse came running in. "What's that barking?" she asked.   201

The con man got down on the floor and growled at her.   213
"Rrrrr." Then he began snapping his teeth.   220

"Oh!" she screamed. "This man has gone mad."   228

The cop ran in. The con man barked at him. The cop said, "I   242
think this man is ready for the rest ★ home."   251

Story above follows Lesson 65

The con man had told the doctor that he was very foxy. The 13

doctor had two helpers lock up the con man. The doctor said, 25

"That man thinks he's a fox now." 32

So the helpers took the con man to a little room at the far 46

end of the yard. They said, "You will like this room. You will 59

have a good time." 63

The con man said, "I am too smart for you. I will get out of 78

this room before the sun sets." 84

But the sun set, and the con man hadn't found a way to get 98

out of the room. He pounded on the floor. He tried to get out 112

the window. But the window had bars on it. And the bars did 125

not bend. 127

At last, the con man sat down on the bed. He said, "I will 141

have to think with my brains. There must be some way to get 154

out of here." 157

Somebody said, "It is easy to get out of here." 167

The con man looked around the room, but he did not see 179

anybody. The con man said, "Maybe I am out of it. I am 192

hearing people talk." 195

Just then the con man saw a foot under the bed. The con 208

man grabbed the foot and gave it a heave. Out came a man. He 222

was smiling. He said, "Hello. My name is President 231

Washington. I am the father of our country." 239

The con man said, "You seem really odd. I don't want ★ to 251

room with you." 254

Story above follows Lesson 65

The con man was in a room with a man who said that he was 15

President Washington. President Washington said that he was in 24

charge of their escape. The con man was just a private in his army. 38

The next day, the president said, "Soon they will come around 49

to feed us. When we hear them at the door, we will zip under the 64

bed. And we will wait without making a sound. Remember to do 76

everything I say, because I don't want anything to mar my plans." 88

"Yes, sir," the con man said. He was very tired. He had 100

marched and marched. He had taken lots of orders from the 111

president. 112

Just then, there was a sound outside the door. "Quick," the 123

president said. "Dart under the bed. And don't let your feet show." 135

The con man darted under the bed. The president darted 145

under the bed. Then the president whispered, "There is dust 155

under this bed, and dust makes me sneeze." 163

The con man whispered, "Don't sneeze." 169

"Hush up, private," whispered the president. 175

The door opened. The con man peeked out and saw two legs 187

walking across the room. Then he saw two more. "Where are 198

they?" a man asked. 202

"Hee, hee," the president whispered. "I can fool them every 212

time." 213

A woman said, "We had better sound the alarm. It looks as 225

if they escaped." 228

The first man said, "But how did they get loose? There is no 241

way out of this room." 246

"I don't know," the ★ woman said. 252

Story above follows Lesson 65

The con man ran from the grove of trees. He jogged up to   13
the president. The president smiled and said, "You see, private, 23
the gate is open. And we are free. Let's run down that road   36
before these yokels come after us."   42

So the con man and the president ran down the road. The   54
people from the rest home ran up to the gate. They said to the 68
gate man, "Did you open the gate and let those men escape?"   80

"Yes, I did," the gate man said. "But the first man had his   93
foot stuck in the gate. He was in pain."   102

"You yokel," the people said. Six people began to run after   113
the con man and the president.   119

"I'm getting tired," the con man said. "Let's stop and rest."   130

"Hush up, private," the president said. "You'll never become   139
a major thinking the way you do."   146

"I don't want to become a major," the con man said. "I just   159
want to get out of here."   165

"Then do what I say," the president shouted. "We're going   175
back to the rest home. Follow me."   182

"What?" the con man asked. "We can't go back. They'll get us." 194

"No, no," the president said. "They don't think that we will go 206
back. That is the last spot they will look. Just do as I say, private." 221

So the president and the con man began to sneak back to the   234
gate. The gate was open. The con man and the president   245
skipped by the gate man. ★   250

Story above follows Lesson 65

The president and the con man were in the bridal rooms of | 12
the big hotel. The president had told the man at the desk that | 25
he and the con man were from the bug company. The president | 37
had said that somebody called about the bugs in the bridal | 48
rooms. | 49

The president said, "This is the life." He sat down on the | 61
bed. "I need something to eat, private. Go down to the dining | 73
room and get a big lunch for us. Charge it to the room." | 86

The con man said, "But I'm not—" | 93

"Hush up, private," the president yelled. "If you want to stay | 104
in this army, you must remember that I am in charge." | 115

"Yes, sir," the con man said. | 121

The con man went down to the dining room and ordered a | 133
big lunch for two. "Charge it to the bridal rooms," he said. | 145

Then he went back to the bridal rooms. The president was | 156
sleeping on the bed. The con man said to himself, "I must get | 169
away from this guy, but I need a plan." | 178

He sat in a chair and began to think. The president was in | 191
the bed, snoring and snoring. Then the con man jumped up. | 202
"I've got a good idea," he said. | 209

The con man ran to the closet. He found a bridal dress in the | 223
closet. He said, "I will put this dress on. Then I will sneak from | 237
this hotel. Nobody will think I am a con man. They will | 249
think ★ I am a bride." | 254

Story above follows Lesson 65

The con man and the president were having lunch in the | 11

bridal room. The president said, "This room is a mess. I | 22

told that bum private to get lunch. But look at the junk he | 35

ordered. Hamburgers and cake. The army just isn't what it | 45

was years ago." | 48

The con man said, "You are so right." | 56

"Yes, my dear. Let me tell you about the battle that we had | 69

some years back. The enemy army had us holed up in a spot | 82

named Valley Forge. We were—" | 87

Suddenly, the president stopped. He jumped up and sniffed | 96

the air. "I smell the enemy," he said. "They are going to attack. | 109

I know it. And I don't even have my army with me. Where is | 123

that private?" | 125

The president ran to the window and looked down at the | 136

street. "There are cop cars down there. We must escape." | 146

The president ran to the closet and came back with dress | 157

pants and a striped coat. He slipped into them. Then he cut | 169

some hair from the con man's wig and made a beard with it. He | 183

stuck the beard on his chin. Then he grabbed a top hat from | 196

the closet. | 198

He looked at the con man and winked. "Don't think of me | 210

as the president," he said. "Think of me as a dashing | 221

man-about-town." | 222

The con man said, "Well, let's dash, buster." | 230

"Who said that?" the president asked. | 236

"Who do you think, buster?" the con man said. | 245

The president began to get ★ red. | 251

Story above follows Lesson 65

The night was cool. Jean looked up at the five moons in the   13
night sky. "I will never feel at home on this planet," she said to   27
herself. She was on night patrol. Her job was to patrol a strip   40
that led from the beach of the red lake to the barracks.   52
Nobody liked night patrol, not with the drams.   60

The drams were little animals that came from the red lake.   71
They looked like grasshoppers, but they were bigger. About three   81
times a year, they came out of the lake. When they did, things   94
got very bad. They ate everything in their path. They ate wood   106
and bricks. They ate the yellow plants that lived on the planet.   118

Last year, they had eaten the barracks. Seven years before   128
that, they had attacked some of the women who didn't get out   140
of the barracks. Nobody could find a way to stop them. The   152
drams moved like a big army, with millions and millions of   163
drams marching and eating, marching and eating.   170

Jean had been on the planet for a little more than six months. She 184
had seen the drams before. One night, they had come from the lake   197
making that "bzzzzzz" that they make. Then they had made their   208
way up the beach to the barracks, eating everything in their way.   220

Then the drams had stopped, just before they reached the   230
barracks. They had stopped going "bzzzzzz." They had   238
been still for nearly an hour. The women had run   248
from the * barracks.   251

Story above follows Lesson 65

For a moment, Jean was frozen as she looked at the drams   12

coming from the lake. She could see them clearly in the   23

moonlight. They were shiny as they moved up the beach.   33

For a moment, Jean didn't remember that she was to signal   44

the barracks as soon as she spotted drams. She wanted to   55

run—run as fast as she could go. She wanted to run as far from   70

the drams as she could get. But she couldn't seem to move. She   83

stared at the drams as they came closer and closer. They were   95

only twenty feet from her now.   101

"Move. Get out of here," she said to herself. But her legs felt   114

as if they had melted.   119

Then Jean began to think. She reached for her signaler. She   130

pressed the button. Lights began to flash in the barracks.   140

Women began to yell, "The drams! The drams! Let's get out of   152

here."   153

And Jean began to run. Now her legs felt like springs. Did   165

she ever run! It was about three blocks from the beach to the   178

barracks, and Jean ran to the barracks so fast that she felt as if   192

she had run only twenty feet.   198

When she got to the barracks, she ran up to the major. Jean   211

was breathing very hard. "Major!" she said. "Major! Major!"   220

The major said, "Take it easy."   226

"Major," Jean said to her, "the drams are coming. They're   236

coming. They're coming up the beach, and we've got to stop   247

them. We've got—" ★   250

Story above follows Lesson 65

The drams were at the other end of the barracks. They had | 12
eaten the wall, and now they were streaming over the floor. | 23
Jean was standing outside the door to Carla's room. Carla was | 34
not in sight. Jean had to get out of the barracks before the | 47
drams reached her. And she had to find Carla. The drams were | 59
coming closer. The "bzzzzzz" was very loud. | 66

Jean ran into Carla's room. She grabbed the trumpet from | 76
Carla's table. "I can make a loud sound with this horn," Jean | 88
said to herself. She took in a lot of air. Then she pressed the | 102
trumpet to her lips. | 106

"Brrrrroooooooooooo," went the horn. | 110

Suddenly the floor shifted. A crash came from the middle of | 121
the barracks. The drams were getting closer. "No time to blow | 132
the horn again," Jean said to herself. "I must get out of here." | 145

She ran from Carla's room. A mass of drams was on the | 157
floor. Jean tried to run past them, but one dram got on her leg. | 171
It bit a hole in her pants. Jean tried to slap it off, and she tried | 187
to run at the same time. Another dram was on her back. | 199

"Ow," Jean yelled. She slapped the dram, and it fell to the | 211
floor. Five or six drams were on Jean now. One got on her | 224
cheek and bit her. A sharp pain shot from her cheek. She hit | 237
the dram, and it fell to the floor. | 245

Now there was a mass ★ of drams on her. | 254

Story above follows Lesson 65

Jean was trying to think of everything that had happened just 11
before the drams went to sleep. She remembered how she had been 23
running with the drams biting her. She ran and fell into a hole in the 38
floor. She remembered getting out of the hole and running again. 49

But were the drams biting her then? "Think, think." 58

"No," Jean said to herself. "I don't remember being bitten 68
after I fell into the hole. Something must have happened before 79
I fell into the hole." 84

Jean tried to think of everything that happened before she 94
fell into the hole. She looked at the beach. More drams were 106
marching closer to the barracks. They were marching over the 116
sleeping drams. "Bzzzzzzzzzzz." 119

"Think, Jean. Think." 122

"I was running from Carla's room," Jean said. "My running 132
couldn't make the drams go to sleep. It must have been something 144
that happened before I ran. What did I do? What did I do?" 157

The drams were very close to the barracks now. "Bzzzzzzzzzzz." 167

Jean started to rub her cheek. She saw that she was still holding 180
Carla's trumpet. "That's funny," she said to herself. "I forgot that I 192
still had it. I must have held on to it when I ran from the barracks." 208

Some of the drams were streaming into the barracks now. 218
"The horn," Jean said. "I gave a blast on Carla's horn. Maybe 230
that's what stopped them." 234

Jean breathed in deeply. Again she pressed the horn to her 245
lips. The horn let out ★ a big blast. 253

Story above follows Lesson 65